F i s h   T o w n

a memoir

John Gerard Fagan

guts publishing

"The whole mad swirl
of everything that was to come
began then."

— Jack Kerouac, *On the Road*

Thank you to my family for their continued support over the years, especially my parents for coming all the way out to Japan. To my brother Michael who has always been the first to proofread my work and give encouragement. To Sophie for everything that's happened since we met. And to Julianne for believing in this book.

— John Gerard Fagan

Fish Town

fish town

only the truly lost wash up on the shore of Yaizu
a fish town in a forgotten part of Japan
faded posters of its 1960s glory days still littering the streets
but that's where I was
April 2013
I took a walk to the sea
hoping for a beach to spend some time after work
but all that was there was a black water port and a tsunami wall
that snaked around it
the Pacific waiting to devour
my flat was behind the destruction line
when the town was flooded I'd be safe
so said the extra 100 quid a month I was told to pay
safe and lost
29 years old
alone
listening to the hum of an air conditioner to drown the silence
I thought I wouldn't last a month
it was over six years before I made the long journey back
home.

the old dreams will sleep

no work in Scotland
graduated right into a recession
on and off the brew
two BAs and an MA led to nothing more than minimum wage
temp jobs
for years
and years
never breaking out of the poverty cycle
first generation in my family to go to university
should have gotten a trade like my father
and his father
and his father before
generations of miners on my mother's side
for years after graduating I survived with work in factories
breaking plastic boxes, packing brochures, sawing wood,
phone monkey jobs for debt collectors and science centres,
hack writing jobs,
and temp bar jobs all over Scotland
nothing more than minimum wage
even tried my luck in London only to eat rejection after
rejection
the stuff of dreams
finally got a decent job with the subtitling-arm of the BBC in
Glasgow
but it was yet another temporary contract, low wage,
unsociable hours
after 18 months I was fed up with the constant worry of if I
had a job by the end of the month
I was in a relationship that was doing neither of us any good

long past its expiry date
fat bursting out from under my chin
unable to sleep
October 2012
03:00
another job hunt online to see if anything had changed in the
last day
teaching English in Asia popped up
as it had a hundred times before
amongst the long list of fruitless courses I did was a TEFL
teaching one
fuck it
nothing to lose
literally nothing to lose but the last strings of my sanity
which would have been lost had I stayed in Scotland
I decided on Japan
memorised as much Japanese as possible in a week
and had a five-minute self introduction perfected
interview in Edinburgh
tricked them into thinking I could speak Japanese
offered a job a few days later
within a few months I had a case packed, sold what I could to
pawn shops,
and headed 5783 miles away.

glasgow airport

I was early for the flight
hadn't slept at all
double, triple checking I had everything
my parents and brother gave me a lift on that dark foggy
morning
we sat in the restaurant at the airport
I had toast and beans but couldn't eat much
all thoughts were drowning and panic simmering
wondering what the fuck I was doing
getting on a flight to Dubai then Osaka
seven years earlier me and Mikey went on holiday to Australia
that was exciting
this just felt like madness
I had no idea where I was going to live or work
just that the company said it was near Tokyo
you can come home at any time my mum said
don't stay out there for the sake of it
I nodded
I checked in and my luggage was too heavy
I had to leave five books behind and a jacket
I exchanged the remainder of my money into ¥
and headed for customs
after months of waiting
the departure had finally come.

japan

I got a teaching job at four wee high schools on a monthly
rotation
thought I was going to a suburb of Tokyo as the lady in the
interview said
but it turned out my new home was in a dying fish town
nowhere near Tokyo
more than four hours away from the city on the local train
and my flat a 40-minute walk to the nearest train station
I was wondering what I got myself into
but fish town had its own wee mountain behind it
gave me something to do before the summer heat arrived
and I burned
and burned
burned.

to feel something

many of us spend our entire lives in hiding
seeking a comfort blanket and wrapping ourselves tighter and
tighter
so we can drift towards old age
in the same town
with the same people
drift and sever anything that goes against that straight path
of comfort
I ripped mine apart
not out of bravery
not out of trying to better myself or the world
I ripped to feel something
anything but grey daylight and grey nights
the stench from the fish factory grounded me into the fabric of
that new town
hardly an upgrade
but it was different
and I needed different.

off the plane

March 22nd
landed in Osaka
a week before I moved to fish town
got off the plane and straight into a taxi
the driver didn't understand a word of my English or broken
Japanese
I showed him a photo of the hotel
he drove me to a police station instead
I was thinking, great it's been five fucking minutes and I'm
getting arrested
but the policeman told the driver where to go
when we got to the hotel the wee driver was delighted he had
found it
happiest face I'd seen in a long time
after the misery of goodbyes
was exactly what I needed.

a room like a spaceship

I went to the 7-11 after I checked-in
gasping for a drink of juice
I picked up a tall can of what I thought was fizzy strawberry
juice
tasted funny but downed it
feeling lightheaded five minutes later I checked the empty can
9% alcohol
I bought three more
and had a shower that waterboarded me from three sides
the room was as futuristic as I had ever seen
white and silver
the toilet was covered in flashing buttons
a heated or chilled seat
and played soothing water sounds
the tv floated down from the ceiling
I sat on the oval-shaped bed and stared out into the neon city
as scared and excited as I had ever been in my life.

suicide on the first train

train to my company induction in Hamamatsu
found a seat and sat in silence
taking in the strange smells and sounds of passing bullet trains
the train was motionless 10 minutes after it should have left
an announcement followed and people flooded off in one wave
I was sure that was the right train
so I stayed put
until the conductor came and ushered the remaining passengers
out
I got off wondering what the fuck to do
a nice old lady explained that someone jumped in front of the
last one and trains on that line were cancelled
after wandering around I found the bus station
four hours later I was in Hamamatsu
a strange city
windy
a backwater compared to Osaka.

mountain school

the week blurred past and I was dropped off in fish town at my
new flat
handed the keys to a small black Toyota
given the list of schools I was working at
and that was that
first day at the first school the following morning
a solid place on the far side of the mountain
new work feeling circled like a shark with the scent of bruised
blood
I parked in an empty space
and waded towards the entrance
the other staff stared like I was the Loch Ness Monster
the only non-Japanese teacher
no one told me everyone had their own space assigned by the
head teacher
so I continued to park there
for almost a month until the nice wee school cleaner told me
that they were all talking about how I was stealing the poor old
maths teacher's space
my real space was a better one closer to the bins
I apologised and said I wasn't told
but that was a huge issue
and one my company received a formal complaint from the
head of English who was meant to tell me where to park
he was also meant to do a school tour and induction
but didn't
showing me my desk was the extent of it
Yosuke Manko
everyone meets someone like him once in their lives

bitter
enjoyed making other people's lives as miserable as his own
there was nothing decent inside this man
nothing
he did little more than bully the weans in his class and
everyone else he had any power over
I'll forever daydream of punching his face.

born in the usa

I was fucked even before I got there
Manko had wanted an American to join their staff
he had a Chad for five years
wanted him back as I took his job when the companies
providing foreign teachers changed
I stood for a good 20 minutes with the reception lady before he
even bothered to tell me where my desk was
she kept trying to get his attention
made everyone feel awkward in the staff room as only he knew
he waited, pretending to be busy
finally as the tension was ready to overflow he slid out of his
chair and stared
pointed to a dusty desk covered in old books
his hands smelt of smoked fish
I soon could tell when he was around from the smell
my first class was in the second period
he asked me to talk about baseball while he watched
I told him I knew nothing about that but I could tell them about
Scotland or football or almost anything else except baseball
he said nope and proceeded to say to the weans I was going to
tell them all about baseball in America
visions of his petty attitude changing burst and ran down the
windows
I played rounders at primary school
so I made it up
not knowing baseball was massive in Japan
I ain't quitting, cunt
I was meant to have two more classes that day
but they were cancelled

I sat in the empty staff room and stared out the window
flies walked about the sill
sunbeams on the dusty cabinets
I stared staying opened-eyed until they watered.

squat

the school was nothing like I had imagined
instead of being futuristic with the latest technology
it was chalk boards and old wooden desks
ancient tvs from the 90s on trolleys like I had in primary
school
nothing had been updated in the school for 20 years or more
I'd later find this was typical of most schools in Japan
not just special to fish town
to top the disaster off the mountain school had only squat
toilets
as far from that Osaka spaceship hotel as possible
I stood over it and had to google how to use it
hoping I wouldn't fall over
my legs cramped up after ten seconds
I could only laugh
it was getting beyond ridiculous there
hot water wasn't a thing either
air conditioning didn't exist
seemed the school budget was spent all on fax machines,
giant printers
and piles and piles of outdated English textbooks.

florida man

Steve was a wee Jewish fella from Florida with long hair and
lip piercings
he landed in fish town at the same time
there were three of us based there for that new semester
the other being Saahd, a fella from England
we split the schools in the wider area
Steve's first week was worse than mine
he had a hole in his trousers
didn't wear any underwear
and his tadger popped out when he was teaching a class
the students were laughing
his face was drained of colour when he told us the story
he didn't last long
was home before the summer ended.

japanese pub

the three of us went to a Japanese pub in fish town on the first
Friday after work
one of the longest weeks of my life
mentally exhausted
I had rationed enough for two pints
pay day still weeks away
and paying up a new flat and flights had maxed out my
overdrafts
but needed a drink
the bar man was real friendly
thought we were fishermen and we told him no different
he opened a tab for each of us to make the bills easy
gave us a bowl of nuts each and refilled when they got empty
encouraged us to play this darts game and even filled it with
coins to keep it on
I was delighted to find a local
feeling relaxed for the first time in months
finished my second pint and went to square him up
expecting to pay a tenner as they were a fiver each
but it was closer to 40
the nuts weren't free
the darts weren't either
there was a table charge for sitting down
lesson learned
never went back.

lawson

jetlag cursed for a good few weeks
wide awake at 03:00
there was a combini called Lawson a minute's walk from my
flat
sold anything you could want 24/7
chips, ice cream, books, shampoo, phone chargers, the lot
I went there those first nights
mainly just to get out for a walk
and try some new food
I ended up going there afterwork most days for a potato
croquette they sold for a quid
and most mornings for a bottle of grape juice for the drive
one of the best things about Japan
24-hour shops and restaurants everywhere
even in long-lost fishing towns.

americans

there was this American lassie who had Scottish ancestry
lived a few towns over
and was at my company's introduction in Hamamatsu before
getting assigned towns
when we were talking she switched into this absurd Scottish
accent
I thought she was joking at first but no
off she went pretending that was always her accent
I didn't know what to do
she meant well but it was beyond awkward
I didn't want to embarrass the lassie but that was just mental
it would have been like me putting on an Irish accent when I
met someone from Ireland
she like many was back home in a matter of weeks.

wounds

some people take their wounds to a foreign land
some place far far away
a new start
can be someone completely new
but an act can only last so long before the real version of
themselves comes out to breathe
and takes over once more
foreign wounds don't heal in a place like Japan
they only get worse, fester, and bleed out
that's why most from the West don't last long
their experience should have been a week-long holiday
two at most.

a fisherman next door

paper walls
23:00 on a Wednesday
he blared salary man porn and grunted along to high-pitched
squealing
I banged the wall thinking maybe he didn't realise the volume
it only got louder
I got used to sleeping with headphones in
I saw him one morning as I went to work
a right wee fisherman
wading boots
whiskers
hair like smoke
stank of cigarettes and dirty water
he left a few months later and the flat lay empty
I hope his ship fucking sank.

monkey time

second school
a fresh start away from Manko
the new teachers were lovely
and unlike Manko were glad to see the back of Chad who I had
replaced there too
really friendly and excited to work with someone from another
country
but there was a catch
at lunch I was told to stop eating and go 'communicate' with
the weans
'practise them the English'
the staff had their faces melted against the windows
watching
I wandered out into the small concrete block
the weans avoided eye contact
I found out I was more of a pet than seen as an equal to the
other teachers
throw it out and let the weans play with it
throw it cos it ain't human
make it dance
make it dance.

dvd

there was a purple DVD shop
between the junior high school and the local primary school
looked strange but I figured I'd pop in after school and pick up
a few Japanese films
to get better with the language
I told my plan to the students in my class and they burst out
laughing
I shouldn't go there they said
it was for adult films only
I thought that couldn't be true
I saw people go in and out there all the time
surely they were joking
I slowed beside it when I drove home
sure enough it had no under 18 signs by the entrance
a fucking porn shop between two schools?
fish town was full of shitty surprises.

fax machines

every day I had to get another teacher to stamp my attendance
sheet
in case the foreigner didn't show up was the logic
and fax this sheet every Friday to be analysed and approved
or I didn't get paid
I hadn't used a fax machine in my life
yet in 2013 I had to learn
all in Japanese
not an email
not a text message
a fucking fax
I started to question why the fuck I was there
more and more
only the scent of the brew in Cumbernauld kept me away.

the local train

went to a live house with Saahd and Steve in Shizuoka city to
watch some rock bands
we had a great night and got invited to stay for the after party
got the last train back to fish town
full of drunken salary men
picking their noses and rolling it into tiny balls
or wiping the wet filth under the seats
an old guy got on later down the track
sat beside me
and placed his hand right on my tadger
I jumped off the seat and he laughed
I restrained from punching his cunt in
no one else on the train did anything except stare
he moved over beside Steve and tried to hold his hand
I thought maybe this was just a weird Japanese thing cos surely
someone would say something
I asked my company and they said it was a problem in Japan
and to report it to the polis if it happened again
lovely
perverts ran wild
while everyone else just watched.

teppie

I got myself into peak fitness running around fish town
nothing much else to do
except sway with the crowds of dust
ran every day for two months with Steve after work after
30 min circuit training
and it paid off for something I didn't even think about out
there
a Japanese guy that worked as a consultant for my company
was also the manager of Teppie
a 4th division football team from the nearest big city
asked me if I played football
he offered me a trial based on my height alone
at the trial I scored four goals and signed for the 2013/2014
season the next day
the Emperor's Cup was my first game in two weeks
one victory away from playing Shunsuke Nakamura's
Yokohama Marinos team
I was thinking this was unreal
never mind the teaching disaster in fish town, I had been
handed the chance to play against one of my favourite Celtic
players
I daydreamed swapping shirts and halving him
things were taking a turn for the better.

we are the world

the school was obsessed with a 1980's song We Are the World
it was sung and studied for fucking months
and had been for years and years
but they took a break from it as something important in the
calendar came up
the school intruder
they practised a knife attack on the school every year
a policeman came into each class with a knife
the teacher armed with a metal pole
they were all to somehow disarm him
could use their chairs, desks, shoes
anything to disarm him
anything
I was not allowed to participate or observe this
and no reason was given why
my classes were cancelled and I was to wait in the locked staff
room
the results were in...
the students froze and the knifeman 'killed' the teacher and at
least two students in every class
Horie the old English teacher was livid
I don't know what they expected from fish town weans
nice wee school though
much better than the mountain one
maybe more 'We Are the fucking World' singing would help
them with the next intruder practise.

earthquake drill

they all practised at the school with yellow helmets and hiding
under the desk
no helmet for the foreigner though
again I was to sit in the locked staffroom as the headmaster
went over the plan in the gym hall
what to do
where to go
I googled my own plan of action
if I was in the mountain school when it happened
I was taking Manko-cunt's helmet.

neko food

Lawson had an offer of 20p cans of tuna in their discount bin
I thought my luck's in here
bought all five cans
decided to have tuna pasta for tea
and the rest for lunch
I cooked the pasta
added sweetcorn
and peeled open a can and tipped it in
it was coated in jelly
I spun the can around
a wee white cat's face smiled back
chucked it all in the bin
I was on the verge of giving up seafood and this pushed me
right over the edge.

umeboshi

old Horie had a 30-year-old batch of salted plums
he was telling me all about them
a real interesting wee fella
with a curiosity about the world outside Japan
I gave him Braveheart to watch and he loved it
didn't know Scotland was its own country
thought it was just a part of England
as most of Japan did
but I set him right and he was a Scottish independence
supporter in no time
so Horie decided he was going to bring the plums in
at lunch in the staff room
he brung out his plums
stood up and did a wee speech about them
and something about his wife and his garden
he offered them to the other teachers but they all refused to
even try
I can still feel the sadness that flowed out from his face
he forced out a trembling smile
I took one and it tasted not bad
he left them on the table
his life's work to be admired
ignored.

teppie debut

players were playing in silence except me
respectful clapping and singing from the crowd
I was playing like a man with a rocket up his arse
screaming for the ball
halving boys
winning every header
tactics were long ball to the big man
but I was playing against ex-pros and some Brazilians
and my last 11s game was when I was 15
but I had been playing 5s and 7s for years
and was at full fitness and could run all day
the opposition were a much better team but I was doing well
best player on my team by fucking miles
half-time whistle went at 0-0
I was confident we'd win
listening to the half-time talk hardly understanding a word
readying to go out and give everything I had
I would never get another chance in my life to play in a
massive game against Nakamura so there was no way I was
losing this
no way no chance no—
the manager finished his speech and turned to me
voice too big he said
next game not so big voice
I was hooked and sent to the stand
team got pumped 4-0.

sunday afternoon

bugs sang in the heat
unknowing
lives full and void of life soaked into the buildings around
sat under the air conditioner on full blast
half-read book by my side
and stared at a yellowed ceiling
silent warmth swallowing fish town
the feeling of being lost blew cold in the room
Sunday afternoon
the day already dying.

lost

Saahd got lost on the mountain that Sunday night
went down a different route and didn't know where he was
I was getting ready for bed when he called to pick him up
hours away from where he should have been
couldn't find his car in the dark
lucky he wasn't alone in the town
or he was fucked
I scrapped my own plans of climbing it the following week
I had a terrible sense of direction
and would no doubt end up in the same predicament
or worse.

mr yesterday

we went to a local ramen shop for dinner the following night
Saahd told me his day at school had been cancelled
and instead there was a staff meeting where everyone had to
apologise on behalf of their head of English, Mr Kino
ol Kino-san had been busy at the weekend
sneaking his camera up the skirts of middle-aged women
and had been for a good few years
he finally got caught by one of the mums at his school
and disappeared from fish town
after the meeting he was never to be mentioned again
swept under the carpet
a popular hobby of Japanese men it turned out
the upskirting capital of the world.

the beach

we bought bikes on Friday payday
mine was stolen a few months later from outside my front door
even though it was chained up
but I got some use out of it
I cycled to find a beach with Steve that Saturday morning
one without a tsunami wall
to see the Pacific
sweating in the white air
we found one a three-hour cycle away
covered in driftwood
smooth grey stones and spits of plastic
black seaweed
the waves were massive
and thundered onto the shore
after almost drowning in India a few years earlier
and in Greece a few years before that
I decided against a swim.

summer in fish town

summer fully arrived with the sound of the cicada
a screaming insect that spat if you went near it
heat dancing off the melting floors
red-dyed roads
no air con at the schools
windows open to let that fresh 40-degree heat circle around the
damp classrooms
a fan in the corner
drenched in sweat every day
appetite long gone
plummeted from a 34 to a size 26.

losing weight

size 28 in jeans were baggy
didn't have much money for food
seven pence noodles and miso powder for most dinners
teaching in the summer heat with no air con or fans was like
being in a steam room for nine hours a day
their solution was open all the windows to let the fresh steamy
air in
winter's solution was also to open all the windows and let the
germs out
the classes were -5 and I had to keep my jacket and scarf on
while teaching
the students were all given blankets
mental
fucking mental.

air con

the air conditioner in my wee flat went on for three hours
then turned itself off
tried everything to change it and keep it on for longer but
nothing worked
this meant in summer I'd wake up in a pool of sweat, stuck to
the sheets, as it turned off during the night
and my room would be a sauna
I got to setting a 04:00 alarm to flick it back on
but that fucked up my sleep
I'd wake up like a damp floor rag
Saahd said his grandfather in Pakistan would pour water on the
floor at night to cool a room
I tried that but with a carpet it didn't help much
I bought a second-hand fan
and positioned it at the end of my bed
but that only blew hot air in my face
in winter it was easier as I'd wake up from the cold
and didn't need an alarm.

mount fuji

a Californian fella called Winn lived a few towns away
he hosted dinner parties at his flat with the five nearest
foreigner teachers
a great cook and all round nice wee fella
he was into hiking, hookers, and shooting fish
maybe that included people too
he was looking for someone to climb the big mountain with at
the weekend
it was something I had on my to do list so we set out a plan for
the Sunday
I got prepared that week and on Saturday stayed in after the
football
and set my alarm for 05:00
we would drive there and start the ascent at 11:00
make it to the top in time for sunset
but he texted as I was going to bed
saying he was told by a teacher at school it was to be raining
and he wasn't climbing in the rain
but the following week he would
the weather app said it was sunny
I held off for a week knowing it would be a mistake
it was 10 degrees hotter that following Sunday morning
Winn had exaggerated his experience with mountains
and came in new shoes that cut his heels to fuck within 10
minutes
but eventually we climbed high above the clouds
and still got to the top for the sunset
at the top I realised I had made a monumental mistake
the skin on my legs had turned pink

I had changed into shorts halfway
forgot to apply sun cream
feeling my legs lock
instead of sleeping at the top as planned I had to get off that
mountain
Winn was too tired to go back so we parted ways
I climbed down in the dark alone
with only my dying phone for light
slipping every five steps on the gravel path
I had no choice as I'd not be able to do it the next morning
took over eight hours to get to the bottom
I drove to a McDonald's carpark and passed out
woke up in a hazy daylight
my legs were purple and blistering
bedridden for days
fever dreams
skin shedded like a snake
perfect start to the summer.

the burning sun

playing football in 45-degree heat was not something I was
prepared for
my face burned even with factor 50 sun cream
I lost strength and couldn't barge boys off the ball like I did in
the first few games
couldn't run with any pace
the team played the Japanese national formation of 4-2-3-1
I asked the manager for more support up front
as I felt I was playing myself most games
and was getting double marked every time
but he changed nothing
by the end of the summer I had lost my place in the team to a
silver-haired 36 year old who had a fag and a Red Bull for his
pre-match meal
he was even slower than me
after being an unused sub or getting 10 minutes at the end I
lost interest in playing
drinking decayed the remainder of my fitness.

a cunt of a marine

Japan was full of American soldiers
a lot in the Yokosuka base a few hours away
I met one marine when I lived in fish town
the boyfriend of an American teacher Branisha from my
teacher training
she was a lovely lassie
but he was a 'the marines have never ever ever ever lost a
battle!' guy
a caricature of an American hero
a crowd of us went bowling
he didn't win
couldn't take it
demanded we play again
saying he was rusty
decided to play by himself right after
and we had to wait on him
just so he could beat the highest score
and show he was the best
we played pool later on
to the same result
Saahd beat him and he was livid
a first-class cunt was all that he was.

yurt

was at this karaoke bar with these American teachers one
Saturday night
we all paid for 'all you can drink'
but all of them had soft drinks
I felt out of place drinking double vodkas while they moved on
to ice cream floats
I lost interest in the conversations and Disney songs
went onto this blue spirit drink next, when this Irish fella
joined the company
he ordered a pint of the blue drink
fucking yanks, eh? he said and laughed
we left them to their singing
and had another 10 at the bar
all cost less than a tenner
the sun was almost up and we were singing Celtic songs
staggering down Hamamatsu main street
still drinking
still laughing
being on the other side of the world you need people you can
relate to at that time in your life
I slept with my head in the bath
guts spilling until the afternoon
but for once it was worth it.

wada

my next school on the fish town rotation was called Wada
a tiny school by the water
that had a few Brazilian and Thai weans whose fathers were
fishermen
they'd read about Japanese castles
I pinned up photos of Scottish castles and was all set to teach
them how to write stories set in an abandoned castle of their
choice
but I was stopped by the next head of English
instead of writing stories he had a much better idea
he moved a chair to the front of the class
and told me to sit
most of the weans had never seen a white person before
and this was a good chance to study what they looked like
the class were to draw me
every class in the school did that week
he meant well
I had 60 drawings on my desk by the next Monday
and I had to pick the winner
they had almost all drawn me as a blonde anime character with
blue saucer eyes
almost 60 identical drawings
the nail that sticks out gets hit on the head.

the electric sun of night

fish town train after work to Tokyo
I was with Steve and Saahd
Shibuya a river of neon
Strong Zero 9% and hot sake wiping out future memories
the sun sandpapered the night away
beyond drunk crawling back at 04:00 into a capsule hotel
the streets were a swamp of restaurant waste
people passed out beside the rubbish dumps
and their guts spilled out beside them
salary men slipping away with the massage hookers
everything seemed just fine when you are floating on a river of
cheap alcohol
just fine
July 5th
I turned 30.

happy birthday

I used to get a happy birthday email from a company that
didn't hire me
I did a phone interview and never heard back until my birthday
seven months later
they always finished their emails with if I knew of anybody
interested in working for them
I didn't block the emails for five years
but hungover in Tokyo on the 6th I finally pressed that button
whispering fuck you into my phone as I did.

hungover in 45-degree heat

guts and organs being squeezed out from the belly button with
every step towards the station
in broken soft pieces
like those pink uncooked insides of chicken nuggets
and there was nothing to be done
but to keep walking
wait it out
and drown in the pain
let it fold and roll until empty
until there was nothing left but a skeleton wrapped in grey skin
and the great sleep opened its eyes and swallowed the rest
the maze that was the Tokyo train system awaited
Saahd had already left early that morning as he didn't drink
and didn't want to waste his day
Steve was in worse condition than me
we fell asleep on the Yamanote circle line
woke up five hours later a few stops from where we started
not even the line we were meant to be taking
got off at Shibuya again and bought three cans of Sapporo
it only made things worse
finally got home hours later
my new decade had started well.

miho

fourth and final school in the rotation
second and third year
teaching them how to write a story set in the past
the first year class teacher Miho wanted to use me as a
recorder for the English textbook instead
she tried to perfect an American accent
told how she practised and practised to sound like a New
Yorker and asked me how it was
it sounded like she was trying an over-the-top Italian accent
but I said it was great and she looked so happy
off to the class she had me read out words
me: aunt
the class repeated
she said no no no and said I said ant - it's auuunt
I tried with the next letter
b - banana
the class burst out laughing
she said it's pronounced ba-nan-ya
and asked me to repeat after her
I said we said things a little differently in Scotland
but we need you to teach them English
yes but I have a Scottish accent and we don't say words
exactly like the Americans or Italians and you might have your
pronunciation slightly wrong on ba-na-na
but we need you to speak English
I looked at the clock on the wall
30 minutes and three more months of her, was it?
auuuunt
bananya

ceeer
dawg...
alefant
no point arguing
gave her what she wanted.

visitors

three paramedics
all dressed like Scorpion from Mortal Kombat
kicked down my door at 21:00 on a Monday night
one had an oxygen tank
the other two a stretcher
wrong door, apparently.

rebels with a cause

a group of boys didn't go to any class
they just hung around the stairs all day
real cool fellas
gelled hair
clasps or bobbles
pink or yellow highlights
they would set off the fire extinguisher and other such mad
shenanigans
done some dance routines
and knew cool words like fuck and shit and bitch
the teachers just ignored them
until an old maths teacher lost the rag and told one to move the
fuck out of his way
the wee fucker hooked him and sent him flying down the stairs
polis were called and that stopped all that
the old teacher never came back
neither did the boy.

opai wassho

a second-year lassie
who instead of going to class would go to the nurse's office
and sleep
she took to sitting beside me when I had free periods
at first she said nothing
but as the days went by she started talking
decided she was going to teach me Japanese
opai wassho was her first lesson
said it was a traditional way to say how are you
and told me to tell the old lady that served the lunches
I did and she burst out laughing
show me your tits I found out it loosely translated to
there ended her days as a Japanese teacher
I found out that she lived in a children's home
her mother had died and her father started a new family
he took her younger brother with him and left her
I wondered what kind of man could do that
turned out that wasn't so uncommon in fish town
the children's home was full.

lunches out of the window

there was a young teacher who had the worst class in the
school
full of other gelled hair boys with pink clasps and bobbles
I was asked to assist him when they were doing presentations
the weans were screaming at each other
he was close to a nervous breakdown
the school lunch got delivered to the classroom
he smiled at me
and asked if I could mind the class for five minutes
by that point they were throwing their miso soup and curry out
the window
one wee fella got control of the teacher's laptop and had hentai
blasting from the tv
I ripped the plug out and walked out
the fuck I was going to be any part of that.

violence

in the staff room on a free period
two first year special needs boys came down
they were sent to ask me to join their class
they were laughing and overly excited practising their hellos
I walked up with them to the oldest English teacher's room
his English lessons were simple
he wrote on the blackboard
they copied
he explained the grammar point in Japanese
nobody learned anything
I got to the class wondering what he wanted
he smiled and said he'd like me to observe his class
he was going to show me how it was done
the two wee laddies were still laughing
he screamed for silence
one couldn't contain his laughter so the old teacher slapped his
head and shook him till his glasses fell off
the class was silent, close to descending into tears
I didn't know what to do
wanted to kick the old cunt's head in
but I glared at him and he pretended like nothing happened
seemed like a common occurrence
I asked him what that was all about and he just sucked in a
breath from his teeth and rubbed his neck
he lived alone near the pier
retired at the end of the year
deserved to die a lonely old man.

lunch thief

there was a fat PE teacher at the school
a right violent wee prick, same as the old English teacher
he would shout and scream and manhandle weans at any
opportunity
the staff lunches were served on trays and left on a long desk
beside the window
it was enough food to feed a child but not an adult,
especially one of his size
there was always extra in the pot
so he would pile all of it into his bowl and take the remaining
bread or rice
on Tuesdays the menu was a Japanese curry, accompanied by a
melon roll and soup
he had filled up his tray to the brim as usual
and went to the toilet
but he left his tray beside the others instead of taking it back to
his desk
everyone always knew which one was his when he did this on
occasion
I was hungover that day and didn't pay any attention
I took the first tray and slumped back into my desk
I remember thinking at last this was worth the money I had
paid for it
it was only when I looked around and caught his eye two
teachers away and saw the pittance he had that I realised I'd
taken his lunch
his face was boiling over, fists clenched
couldn't do anything about it by then
I apologised after saying I didn't realise it was his

he didn't even blink
well go fuck yourself then
I thought about swiping his lunch again the next day but I had
enough enemies
all was forgotten in a few weeks
he even bought me a souvenir from the school trip to Kyoto.

page 3 fellas

any combini I went to in the morning
there would always be a few fellas standing by the magazine
stand
giving the latest porn a good look
not an ounce of shame as school weans brushed past them to
get their breakfast
this wasn't just a fish town thing
I'd see this all over Japan.

ageha

Saturday night
took six hours to drive to Tokyo
Steve didn't feel confident enough to drive so I was left with
all the responsibility
we took the wrong turn three times
and had to pay a tenner for every mistake to get back on the
motorway
parked in a supermarket
dumped our bags at this mental American lassie's flat
Steve had met her on the plane over
she'd been over to fish town to visit him the week before
we'd slept on her floor when we went to Ozzfest a few months
earlier
with the bags dumped, we got a bus to this big nightclub called
AgeHa
it had its own beach and pool
another American fella, a friend of the lassies, came out too
he had been in Japan for a few weeks longer than us
said he had a master pick-up line for Japan
he pointed to himself and said, American!
that was it
said I should try it
not to say Scotland
as no one there knew where the fuck that was
I should always say I'm American
he looked like he was psyching himself up for a match at
WrestleMania instead of a night out
things took a bad turn before we even got in
the lassie who we were meant to be staying with

and who was winching Steve the whole way over
fucked off with a new fella in the queue
Steve was understandably dumbstruck
didn't see her till 05:00 at the train station
she had no money to get back home
he paid for her ticket
we got our bags, crashed out for a few hours in the car park,
and drove home
he fell asleep holding the map on his phone
took nine hours.

japanese lessons

there were free Japanese lessons to the foreigners in fish town
on Friday nights
with nothing much else to do I went with Saahd
there were a few Filipino, Brazilian, and Indian immigrants
and some weans came to draw and play games
like a nice wee community centre
the teachers were retired Japanese ladies in their 80s
one of them took to teaching me
she spoke zero English
I spoke almost zero Japanese except a self-introduction
and random words
but we tried and she was as kind as can be
the old ladies would bring in all kinds of food and baking for
us to try
always filling the tables with food
it wasn't what I pictured my Friday nights to be like
but I liked it
and hardly missed a lesson.

first band

Steve was a drummer in a band back in Florida
so we decided to start a band
inspired by watching the Japanese bands in Shizuoka city
we went to Hard-Off, a second-hand superstore a few towns
away to get started
you could get everything in there
the size of a big Asda but full of electrical junk and old clothes
I bought an electric piano
he bought a drum kit
we wrote two songs and recorded them
even played with Wemmer, the band who headlined the gig we
saw the month before
it could have went somewhere
but like most things it died on its arse
as he decided to go home.

homesick

after four months Steve is homesick beyond repair
his ex-girlfriend pregnant and might be his
oldest trick in the book
missing out on life back in Florida
I was gutted
gutted
he was the first friend I made that left
almost everyone I met in my first year left soon after
temporary and constantly changing friendships in Japan would
become draining
but something that came hand in hand with living in a way
station.

two remained

after Steve left, Saahd was the only other person I knew in the
town
we would meet up for Japanese lessons on Friday
then go for pizza in Fujieda in the next town over
since my Japanese was weak he'd be the first person I'd
properly speak to all week
he didn't drink, which was good for me
he spent the rest of his weekends studying at a coffee shop
keeping himself to himself
and got a weekly hair trim from a Japanese lassie he fancied
I sometimes joined him for a weekend wander around
Shizuoka city
a 40-minute drive away
I wouldn't have survived without his company in fish town.

the pictures

I went with Saahd to watch Gravity in the city
hadn't seen a film in the pictures for months and was really
looking forward to it
I used to have an unlimited Cineworld pass back in Glasgow
and go at least once a week
I presumed the film would be subtitled in Japanese
I presumed wrong
George Clooney was floating around in space
his music in the spacesuit was in English
then he spoke in a deep Japanese voice
Subarashii
Saahd burst out laughing
great
luckily there wasn't much dialogue in the film
turned out the Japanese loved a good dub.

tsuki

I went out with this Japanese girl at the turn of the season
lasted longer than it should have
but she lived hours away so it suited me
and as a tour guide she could not be faulted
met on a trip to Kyoto
she gave me directions
and her number
she was 25 and as Japanese as they came
she was going to get married through an old Japanese
matching system
find herself a rich husband to take care of her
like her mother did
she had a fucked up view of what a relationship was
acted like she owned me
before we were anything more than friends
jealous over everything
anything.

onsen

her idea for a first date was to go to an onsen since I had never
been to one before
I didn't see the point as they separated male and female
but I went to see what's what
there were rock pools full of different minerals and colours
in them or hanging out them were an assortment of naked
Japanese fellas
mostly ancient figures
I sank into the first pool where there wasn't many people
an old guy sat on the rock by my shoulder
and proceeded to talk to me in Japanese
with his baws dipping into the water
everywhere I looked eyes were on me
staring like vampires
and I had stumbled into their lair
I had never felt so uncomfortable in all my life
I made sure the next time I went to one that it was not at a peak
time.

kobe zoo

thousands of monkeys crammed into a cage
people were all slapping the cage
making the monkeys scream and curl up into the centre
Tsuki joined in with the cage slapping in a fit of giggles
there was a bear in an enclosure no bigger than a couch
an elephant and giraffe glued to an ash pitch together
she loved it there
hated the Chinese
wouldn't wear anything or eat anything made in China
it was poison
they were all poison
every single one of them
Tsuki
she had a beautiful name
I'll give her that.

burning man

two American teacher lassies said they had heard the Burning
Man festival was coming to Japan
three-day event
me and Saahd got tickets and drove the seven hours to get
there
the Americans wanted to car share
but were popping all the pills and had a car full of drugs
fuck that
one of their boyfriends had even sent over MDMA from
America in a pick n mix
the polis would have locked her up for good if she got caught
mental lassie
absolutely mental
risking life in jail
in a ruthless country when it came to drugs
we got to this abandoned beach
an array of American army folk on leave and Japanese who
worshiped anything American
first night they burned these wooden figures
foam party on the beach
the American lassies were rolling around crying on the sand
one was dressed up in a homemade cat costume
I had some warm sake and was projectile vomiting and went to
bed early
but it was only Friday
Saturday was the big night
in the morning half the people had left
the organiser told us that the local fisherman needed the beach
back as some special fish had swam into the bay

the event was cancelled

no refund

they played Full Metal Jacket on a big screen for the remaining
people

a topless American offered us cold fatty bacon from a plastic
lunchbox

she looked like she hadn't washed in a year

teeth damp with rot

I kindly declined

the perfect ending to a perfect weekend.

karigane festival

October
an Irish lassie called Leanne came to the Japanese lessons
and said she had been invited to a fire throwing festival where
she taught and asked if me and Saahd wanted to come
we went and it was exactly that
there were massive poles with straw baskets on top
filled with fireworks
I was given a helmet and a chain with a lump of straw doused
in petrol
it was set alight
everyone was swinging the chains and firing their torches
trying to set the baskets on fire
fireballs were everywhere
I had a shite aim and almost hit someone a few times
almost got hit in the face with a fireball a few times too
the craziest legal festival I had ever seen
deadly
people not participating were holding water buckets to douse
those caught on fire
after the three towers were lit everyone watched as they burned
down
and got drunk
I was interviewed by a Japanese tv company
I still knew fuck all Japanese
but knew enough to tell them it was great.

nov 2013

my twin brother Mikey visited
the only one from home that did while I lived in fish town
was my best week since I moved
he got off the plane
suitcase lost in Amsterdam at the connection
I was being pestered by a camera crew wanting to follow us
around and film us going about Tokyo
told them to fuck off in the nicest way possible
headed to a Uniqlo and he bought a change of clothes
checked into a traditional hotel in Shibuya
and headed out for a drink
his case didn't turn up until three days later
but that didn't ruin the trip.

akb42

on the way back from playing old arcade games in Akihabara
we passed the AKB42 concert hall
a girl group with a thousand members that sang shite songs
the shows were going on every few hours
for a laugh we decided to go watch one
but in the queue was only old men in their 50s and 60s
all in their smoky business suits
creepy as fuck
I left feeling I'd seen another side of Tokyo that I didn't need
to see.

shibuya

did the usual tourist traps in Shibuya
and met Mark and Ricky at the big crossing
did a good pub crawl
that finished in Womb
a club that drew me in several times over the years
even though it was a shithole
ramen called at 04:00
and crawled into the big capsule hotel in Shinjuku
my alarm blared at 09:50
head feeling like a balloon full of razors
when we were on holiday in India
after I finished up with the debt collecting job
we got caught up with a heroin smuggling gang
and were lucky not to have been killed
but I would have traded that for an extra hour in my bed
10:00 checkouts were the worst
there were pools of vomit from some American tourists who
dangled out from their beds
the bumpy train to Disneyland had me thinking I'd do the
same.

tokyo disneyland

little did I know I'd be living near there four years later in
Urayasu
went on all the rides
on space mountain we both realised we were done with
rollercoasters
after bungee jumping and skydiving 10 years earlier
the thrill from a wee rollercoaster was gone
only a sickening feeling from having your baws rattled
remained.

the mountain

we stayed in fish town for a few days as I had to work one day
I took him to the port
palm trees blew in the wind
the grey tsunami wall
a drifting dust of silence
he wondered what the fuck I was doing out there
we climbed Mt Takakusa
fish town's only attraction
sun soaked with no wind
out of breath and out of water we reached the summit
worth it for the pale view of Mt Fuji and the coast
Mikey said if he lived there he'd go every weekend
I should have went more often
but I spent most weekends getting drunk or getting out of fish
town.

tokyo

Tokyo was a different kind of wilderness
went back there for his final few days
I asked Mikey if he could ever live there
I knew the answer before he told me
he had just broken up with his girlfriend
a lucky escape as she would have given him a hard life
we had a great week
but I could see the depression dripping out his face at the
thought of returning home
even then he wouldn't have traded for my new life in the far east.

lost in translation

we went to the New York bar that Lost in Translation was
filmed in
exact same setting
even a jazz singer just like the film
we got a table that gave us a stunning view of the city
I felt the magic of that city pouring in
the unique lights and sounds and smells all far below
roads full of red or white lights
purples, blues, and pink neon dotted around every corner of
every building
the lives of 36 million others
entwined
a good place to start or end a night out
but one I never went back to again
I never planned not to
but looking back it would only have ruined the moment.

earthquake

last day
sleeping 15 floors up
biggest earthquake of the year
the guy in the capsule above me leapt out and ran down the
stairs
the building swayed as if we were on a ship at sea
I was too hungover to panic
the airport line was damaged
so Mikey had to get three trains
lucky we were early
if Japan taught me anything it was always be early
if you are on time you are late.

start of winter

windows all wide open in the school
to let the germs out I was told
weans sitting under blankets
frozenjawed and silent
and expected to write
learn
and be happy
madness.

football career ended

by the middle of winter I was back in the first 11 but nowhere
near match fit
at a corner I was elbowed in the mouth and given a penalty
I was all set to take it when the ol silver-hair Red Bull fuelled
fella ran past
and sent it flying over the bar
I stared with blood dripping over the pink strip
in the second half I beat three players and set up the winning
goal
but it felt like a defeat
my only man of the match award
skin coated in sweat and ice
I lost all desire to play
the team narrowly avoided relegation
I finished the season but turned down a new contract
I wasn't getting paid much as my visa was for teaching only
my short football career was over.

dead of winter

every morning I'd wake up frozen needing a hot shower to de-
thaw
since the air-con kept turning off and I had no money to buy a
heater
I filled up a glass bottle with boiling water one Monday
and it cracked and soaked my bed in the middle of the night
slept on the floor
wearing three layers of clothes
watching the clock tick
02:00
03:00
04:00
05:00.

long hours

schools ended at either 15:30 or 16:00
but everyone in all the schools stayed late
pretending to work
just for show to the headmaster
they were so unproductive
and masked it in crazy long hours
some not leaving the school until 21:00 some nights
they seemed surprised when the last bell rang I was out
my lessons were all planned
no reason to stay unpaid.

enkai

I was invited to the end of year staff night out at my second
school
they were surprised as fuck when I accepted
it was at a wee izakaya near the train station in Fujieda the next
town over
I was sat beside the maths teacher
a young fella in his 20s who could speak English
he talked about how he was just married and his wife was
learning English and how excited he was to be starting a
family
he invited me over to their house for dinner the following week
the other teachers were teasing him about being a newly wed
especially the school secretary
a big woman in her 50s with a face overcooked in childish
makeup
I tried my best to join in conversations
but my Japanese was limited and the wee maths teacher soon
stopped translating
and focused his full attention on the secretary
they left hand in hand soon after
one of the English teachers said it was a rule that no one brings
up anything that happens on the work night out so don't
mention that to him tomorrow
it was a sleepy fish town not Las fucking Vegas
I paid up, got the train,
and walked the 40 minutes back to my flat
before I got dragged into some swinger's party.

licence plate

Christmas break I drove to Himeji to meet Tsuki and see the
big white castle
one of those moments when it sunk in that I was in Japan
driving took more than eight hours
but was half the price of the train
on Christmas Eve I went to Kyoto to meet Saahd and his wee
pal from England
we stayed in a hostel that had a big pub connected to it
almost everywhere was closed
but we found a ramen shop and had dinner
plan was a quick shower, change, and out to the pub
the place was bouncing by the time we got back
I went to my company car to get my towel and noticed the
license plates had been stolen
I told the hostel and they said I couldn't move it without plates
against the law
it was on a meter
I was fucked
just wanted to get drunk and deal with it in the morning but the
polis had been called
this wee polis fella interviewed the hostel staff and concluded I
had stolen them
and I was going to get fined
I asked him why I'd steal my own plates
maybe I collected them was the answer
there was cctv in the car park so I told the cunt to look
twitching with anger
he did but the cameras were mysteriously broken
he left right after and the case was closed I was told

so that was no doubt a lie
he just knew it wasn't me who did it and wasn't going to take
it any further
I emailed my company
they arranged for it to be towed back to fish town for 500 quid
at my expense
I didn't have 500 quid so this was changed to a lady would
come tomorrow with new number plates
instead of going to Nara on Christmas day I waited all day at
the hostel to meet this woman
she turned up at 17:00
I screwed the plates back on and left
driving back was the first time since arriving I felt
homesickness overflowing.

decision time

pay was half in August and December
I still had a loan out with the company
credit cards maxed
overdraft maxed
living on 12¥ noodles for months
towards January I thought about staying a second year
everyone in Scotland thought I would be long since home by
then
my brother said if I didn't come back, I'd be forgotten about
everyone was getting used to life without me
getting married
starting families
and it would soon be too late to return
I used to have dreams about being home
and homesickness would claw at my gut for days after
but there was nothing in Scotland for me
I had a job in fish town
I was in a routine
in many ways I liked it there
preferred it even
so I renewed for a second and final year.

fish town routine year two

my routine had improved going into year two
Monday night 5-a-side with fellas from my former football
team
Tuesday night yoga
Wednesday night taught Saahd piano in my flat
Thursday straight to bed after school to catch up on sleep
Friday night Japanese lessons with Saahd and Emily
Saturday either drinking with Mark in Hamamatsu or spending
the day writing
Sunday worked on my writing during the day and studied
Japanese at Emily's
I was busy
work was easier
the mountain school still hell but I only had to go there for two
months of the year in total.

far beyond demise

Saturday nights frequently consisted of getting hammered with
Mark
and heading to Marty's bar where he lived in Hamamatsu
a good two hour's drive from fish town
I met Ivan on a night out
big long-haired fella from Paraguay
asked me if I was in a band
he was a guitarist
and just recently lost his singer in his band
metal music
I'd never scream singed before
but thought fuck it might as well
I looked up online how to scream
practised after school in my car near the empty pier
an audition at a karaoke bar the following Sunday
a few hours later I was in a new band
Far Beyond Demise.

first gig

at a rehearsal studio mucking around
met Renato the bass player from Peru
practised a few covers
Metallica, Pantera, Slipknot
Ivan said it was sounding good
asked if I want to jam in another place later with those songs
just a few of his friends would be there
fuck it why not
we drove to a venue
and there were over a thousand people
he said we were on third in the line-up
and introduced me to the others in the band
I was thinking, whit?
we had hardly practised
best way to see if I was any good
I was pissed off as he said our first gig was in a month
I hardly remembered any of the words
a few pints later we were up
I could hardly see anyone from the stage as the lights were so
bright
I closed my eyes
pictured I was in Wallace's army at Stirling Bridge
and felt the adrenaline course through
the drums and guitar started
and I screamed my lungs out
revolution is my name
I thought I did fine
until Marcos said I should watch myself in the mirror
I was all over the place

but vocals were good
I had only ever played gigs solo with a piano
and wasn't used to having nothing in front of me
but overall a decent start to the new style.

jlpt

after months of studying I passed the Japanese language exam
along with the lessons on Fridays
I studied at Emily's flat with Saahd on Sundays
then we'd watch a Japanese film or tv show
Emily was French
we met at the Japanese class at the end of my first year in fish
town
married to a Japanese Uruguayan
another lost in fish town
her husband worked nights at a factory
she worked at a nursery
a kind lassie
we did yoga on Tuesdays together
Japan got too much for her once she had a baby
but she went back after only a year home in France
no work for her husband there
he'd left Uruguay after getting robbed at gunpoint
their only hope was in Japan.

rain

I heard how bad monsoon season was
but I liked it
I'd wake up to find a message saying school was cancelled
stay indoors
there are few better feelings of being sleep deprived and
getting an unexpected day off
with the sound of wind and rain beating on the window
a country boy American teacher a few towns over was one of
the thickest people I had ever met
he went out driving in a monsoon and broke down
the company went mental at him
he figured it was a nice time to get out
and not waste a free day off
he also found a dead body while running around a lake in
Fujieda a few weeks later
I never heard of him after that.

a mouth on fire

a summer night out with Mark at Marty's bar
still drinking cans of 9% at 06:00
Mark's flat didn't have aircon
passed out in the living room with no fan
woke up in a pool of sweat still steaming
went for a CoCo curry for breakfast
ordered the hottest curry possible
I usually had a 2 in extra spice and that was hot
ordered a 10 and coated it in more chilli flakes
I was halfway in munching away when the hangover hatched
mouth on fire
felt like I was floating up to space
tongue swelling
eyes streaming
I drank two jugs of water
and three melon pan loafs from the combini
took almost a week to recover
30 years old
reverted to drinking like I was 18 again
once back in fish town I lay in the bath until it turned cold
I had spent my weekly food budget on one night of drinking
I went to the ¥100 shop and chose three items to last me until
Friday
Mark got a new job and left for Tokyo not long after
the big city was my aim from the start
but wasn't easy to get a job there with weak Japanese.

ivan's birthday

things were going well with the band
we had a set sorted and a good few gigs under our belt
we played a gig on his birthday
then to the usual pubs in Hamamatsu
and after to Ivan's house party at around 03:00
I was 'spinning when I closed my eyes' drunk by then
I got a taxi with Winn
found his block of flats
crawled up to the second floor and kicked his door
it swung open
I blazed inside and headed for the living room expecting a
horde of South American metal heads
the flat was ghost quiet
sitting on the couch swigging a can of Strong Zero I realised
we were in the wrong flat
his building was two over
I sprinted out faster than I've ever ran in my life
by the time we got to Ivan's I had sobered up
no doubt the owners were petrified and had called the polis
I had to kerb this excessive drinking
no longer in my 20s
instead of stopping I drank a mix of vodka and rum until I
passed out on the kitchen floor
I walked with Winn a good hour back to the train station in the
last breaths of morning.

2014 independence referendum

they put tvs in the staff room for important news events
Scotland's vote on independence was one of them
I voted via proxy with my brother
I had been talking about it in my classes and to the other
teachers
certain we would win
and Scotland would be free
there was cake and drinks organised for a celebration
I was excited
but when the results came trickling in I could feel the colour
drain from my face
I just finished a class and got down to hear the final news
I slumped into my chair
couldn't move
what the fuck was wrong with people back home?
that they would vote against their own independence from a
tyrannous neighbour?
for the first time I felt lucky to be thousands of miles away.

jun monogatari

started writing my first Japanese story
I was a man living in a decaying fish town
its glory years long behind it
so it started with that
from a Japanese factory worker's perspective
and the feeling of loneliness
and let the story wander
and wander
into a novel.

which or that

Manko invited Chad back to do a demo lesson at the mountain
school when I returned
and asked the head teacher to watch
Chad had hung about in the nearest city wanting his old job
back
I knew Manko's game but could do fuck all about it
Chad was going to do the first half of the lesson
then I'd do the second
he asked me to prepare a 'which or that' worksheet
said Chad was doing something similar
and the lessons would gel
I made one and he asked for it to be harder
so I changed it
perfect he said and printed it
that Friday comes
he actually played fucking entrance music for Chad
and the two of them were dancing
they played a game of Blockbusters on the board with music
and the weans loved it
like a wee party
and he gave out chocolate and prizes right after
I said to him I'd continue this kind of lesson with a quiz so just
keep them in their teams
he ignored that
and cut the music and said, John-sensai wants us all to do a
worksheet now
the chocolate was to go away
the weans were livid
he was apologising as if it was all my idea

he handed out the 'which or that' worksheet and said I
demanded silence
asked me to explain it
half the weans were asleep
it was way above the level they were at
after about three minutes he collected the worksheets and
mouthed 'too hard' to the headmaster and handed them back to
me.

st patrick's parades

started in Yokohama on Saturday afternoon
a small parade led by an old white fella dressed up as St
Patrick and Miss Ireland 1989
Mark had signed us up to be part of it and we got a free t-shirt
and a pint of Guinness
I was given the Dublin flag to wave
as none of the real Irish folk wanted to touch it
Mark and Ricky had their own county's
I hated Guinness
hadn't drank it since I was 17
but had ten cans during that parade
then the real drinking began
didn't get home till 07:00
up at 09:00 for the bigger parade in Omotesando
I had agreed to walk with the Tokyo Celtic supporters club
my head louping
the shakes drumming my bones into the concrete
Mark gave me what I thought was a bottle of coke
I drank a good chunk
it was almost pure whisky
but it sorted me out for a few hours
I got back to fish town late that evening looking and feeling
like a dug-up corpse
by the following Sunday I would be gone from Yaizu
never to return.

flat

Leopalace Astrea I
room 206
Higashikogawa
the first place I could call my own
for the first time in my life
no sharing a bedroom or bathroom or kitchen
it was cramped
my head almost at the ceiling
sweltering in summer
freezing in winter
the only window opened out to a factory
that wafted over the scent of dried fish flakes
but it was mine
and somewhere when I close my eyes
I can still see, feel, and remember in all its detail
oversized 1990s tv
yellowed fridge
tiny beige table and single chair
the wire brown carpet
cream walls
with still some light left inside
fish town's first and likely last Scottish resident.

fish town no more

two full years had passed in fish town
I decided to stay a third and final year
then salvage something of a life back in Scotland
Tokyo was on my mind and I thought I'd regret it if I never
lived there
but I was settled in fish town
I had good friends around
my band was getting good and were close to getting on a tour
I had a month-long spring break between the semesters
I paid the rent for the oncoming month
filled up the car
made plans to go to Hong Kong for a week
I was all set
on a Sunday night I was at the local supermarket getting a food
shop in
my phone rang
it was the ex-army American boss of my company
Hans fucking Richter
he looked and sounded like his name
he said to call him back once I was back in my flat
I finished my shopping and drove home
I hate phone calls
fucking hate them
it was going on 21:00 so something must have been up
but thought nothing of it
maybe he was just calling to confirm my position for the next
semester
or I had missed some paperwork
I put the food in the fridge and called him back

he said Manko from the mountain school had made a long list
of complaints
I wore aftershave (I didn't even have any)
my hair was too long (it was cut short)
students were wearing blue contact lenses (so I had to wear
sunglasses to cover my eyes?)
I didn't high-five enough (whit?)
my lessons were boring (he decided what I would teach and
didn't approve of any of the creative writing classes that I did
at the other schools)
I didn't engage with the kids enough with things that they liked
(oh I fucking did. I brushed up on all that Kyary Pamyu Pamyu
and Yokai Watch shite)
I dressed too smart (I was told to wear a shirt and tie and I did.
Did he expect me to come to work in my fucking jammies?)
my lessons were too hard (only the which or that worksheet
was and was all his idea)
this list went on and on
Hans heard my case and probably knew it was all a lot of shite
but said sorry it was too late
my job and apartment had already been given to an American
fella who will be more suitable
he said I was welcome to stay with the company as I had
signed a new contract
I could either go to a school 'near' Kyoto or go fuck myself
I said I'd only stay if I could get a placement in Tokyo or it is
option two
so to be fair to the fella he made a few phone calls
and by Monday night offered me a new set of schools in
Tokyo near the airport
I agreed
although sad to be leaving fish town
finally getting to live in the big city brought with it a sense of
excitement.

nowhere near tokyo

Tokyo is a massive metropolis
after living in fish town for two years, living in the thick of it
was something I wanted to experience
I waited and waited on my new address to be emailed
I was packed up and ready to go
the night before I had to move out my email pinged
my new flat was in a town called Shisui
I googled it
not in Tokyo
nowhere near fucking Tokyo
papped out into another wilderness in rural Chiba nowhere
near anywhere
a good two hours on several trains away from Tokyo
a 50 min drive away from Narita airport
a Tokyo airport by name but nowhere near the actual city
rural as fuck
I should have gone home
but I was still in debt and stubborn that I was leaving on my
own terms.

shisui

the new town had a McDonald's that closed at 18:00
a clothes shop that closed at 17:00
100 yen shop
and nothing much else
two train stations were positioned on either end of the town
took 15 minutes to walk the whole town
I had a ground floor flat this time
similar size to the one in fish town
looking out to a derelict piece of land full of crickets, spiders,
and a mikan tree with rotting fruit surrounding it.

16 days

Saahd helped me move to Shisui
we had hung out two-three times a week for two years
and now that was over
I was a seven hour drive away from fish town
I only ever saw him a few times again after that
when he left I got to organising my new flat
which took all of 20 minutes
I still had the gap between semesters off in spring
but now no money to go anywhere
I walked around the clothes store for something to do
walked an hour to the re-use factory to buy a ¥100 t-shirt
walked hours in the sun to get to Narita
and wandered around the big shrine
statues
ponds coated in slime
when my wages came in 16 days later
I got the train and met Mark in Bic Camera in Tokyo
took me a while to get used to talking again
and fight the desire to go home, lock the door, and curl up
under a blanket.

a dry stick in a basket

if you want to feel real loneliness
move as far away from your home country as possible
to a small town with nothing around
still be learning the language
know a few people
but they are either too busy to meet or too far away
wander around alone
with little money left
don't speak to anyone in days
weeks
work boring, unfulfilling
eat alone
live alone
smile and say thank you when buying ramen from the local 7-
11 the extent of your conversations
sleep no more than a few hours at a time
watch as your mental health crumbles.

pink car

the company gave me a small pink car to get to the new
schools
dropped it off at 07:00 and fucked off while I was sleeping a
few days before I was to start
great
just fucking great
that was all I needed
a giant white man in a pink car coming to teach at your school
I called them after the first day as I got comments from the
teachers
the company said the cars were selected at random from the
dealership and nothing could be done
I decided I'd crash it and get a swap
I knew someone had done that before and got a new
replacement
if my luck was out and the replacement was pink then so be it
the night before I decided to clip an old wall at the end of my
street, I got a call saying a girl a few cities over had asked for a
pink one
so I swapped with her
and got a brand new silver Suzuki Wagon R
a great wee car
best I'd ever had
things were looking up.

demise

after moving to Shisui
the band wasn't practical for gigs on the weekend in
Hamamatsu or beyond
I went back once a few months later and our gig was cancelled
at the last minute
I drove back to Shisui that Sunday night knowing that it was
over
Ivan started Dime Fest, a live-house monthly event
aimed for us to headline it
but I was a 10-hour round trip from there
adding up the petrol cost and the effort only resulted in one
thing
it was a great experience
but it couldn't work
my time in the band was over.

yokai-chiba

assigned to a special-needs school
a four-hour drive from the flat in Shisui
I didn't have to do anything, they said
just turn up and interact with the weans
and there would be training provided for the first week
and on-going training after that
I got there early
and the whole school was already in a gym hall waiting
there was about 50 kids and 10 teachers
the headmaster introduced me to them to a big clap
then the teachers all left and looked in from the corridor
through a window
I went to leave and the headmaster smiled and said, 30 minutes
please teach, anything okay
then he fucked off to the window
I took out my phone and played 500 miles on loop
and took it from there
played any game that came into my head
mainly guessing games where they chose a corner
lovely weans
but that should never have happened
I presume my company lied to them that I was some kind of
specialist
or maybe they just didn't care
I managed to make a success out of that first day
when it could have went very fucking wrong.

kenji sawada

at the special needs school
had to sit in a computer room when I wasn't teaching
a few 20-year-old PCs on two dusty tables was all that was in
there
I was stuck there from 9-4 and taught for one hour at most
having a six-hour paid break was not a bad gig at all
gave me time to plan lessons for the other schools, work on my
novel, and practise Japanese
a wee orphan boy who looked like a stuffed rabbit that had
been in a loft for 30 years
came and sat beside me in the late afternoon and stayed until
home time
and returned every week after
he liked to show me videos on YouTube of Kenji Sawada
an old singer from the 1960s/70s
Kenji Sawada, he said and sat in silence smiling at the screen
I was told that was his mum's favourite singer and they used to
listen to him together
he liked lists too
if I named any video game he told me the year it was made
I listed the arcade games I used to play at the Millport
amusements when I was a wean
knew them all
all the Super Nintendo and PlayStation games I ever played
knew them all
then more Kenji Sawada
same routine every time
poor wee fella
I liked my time with him

no one else paid him much attention
but they were understaffed
with a lot of weans needing much more help
a tough job for the people working there
all trained as normal teachers
but was up to the council who got moved there.

chiba wilderness

drove through miles and miles of roads
cutting through rice field after rice field
sometimes hardly ever saw a car
some small roads backed up on both sides
hours upon hours
in the farmlands of Chiba
the schools would appear out of nowhere
two CDs when the radio signal failed and I had no phone
signal
Frightened Rabbit and Biffy Clyro
on loop in the Chiba wilderness.

shisui routine

ate alone
drove home after work and would choose a cheap restaurant to
eat on the way back
a cook-it-yourself Korean style BBQ a five min drive from
home was my usual on Monday
other days I'd drive half an hour to the outskirts of Narita city
to Sushiro
and sit by the counter and look at 9gag and Celtic rumours on
my phone
then buy some chocolate almond balls at the Family Mart
beside it
it was a boring life
but money was coming in and my debts were almost paid off.

all ready to retire

I had a high school on Mondays
Togane
none of the English teachers were under 60
they liked to practise their English with me
and ask all the questions
lovely people
genuinely all nice people which was rare
they all fell asleep at their desks at lunch time
didn't take long for me to join them in that custom.

narita-seriyou

the parking space was under a tree that coated the car in shite
a school for high school weans who were going to work in
factories or the likes
zero interest in English or writing any kind of stories I was
warned
which was fair enough
and none of them could speak a word
boys and girls separated
and I was given the oldest boys' classes
around 10 in each
they'd all sit with their phones out, drink Red Bull, and eat
crisps
not giving two fucks about anything
the school said I could do whatever I wanted
I had watched the last episode of Salad Fingers the night
before so I played them episode one
then they could go do their own Salad Fingers comic strip in
English
worked a fucking treat
by the end of the class they could all say that they liked rusty
spoons
absurd cartoons it was for the rest of the year
I lined up Ren and Stimpy, Charlie the Unicorn, and Don't
Hug Me I'm Scared
some just spent the whole time drawing Salad Fingers or
Stimpy
but most had found a way in to learning the language.

pachinko

I went for one run in Shisui
and after a minute I realised my fitness was back to zero
I jogged along a walkway on the side of the dual carriageway
gasping for breath
filthy clouds of mosquitoes were foaming out from the bushes
and chasing after me
faded to a walk after 10 minutes
and continued until I came to this abandoned pachinko parlour
I'd passed driving to work
yellow paint flapping from the walls
weeds poking through the roof and swaying in the cracked
concrete garden
a strange building
out of place
exactly how I felt in that town.

schools

going somewhere different everyday was mentally exhausting
with at least four different classes over three year groups in
each school
soon I had no idea where I was with any of the classes
Monday Togane shogyo
Tuesday Tomisato
Wednesday Narita seriyou
Thursday Yokai Chiba
Friday Matsuo
none were under an hour's drive from the flat I was given
that wee car did some amount of miles
ready for the bin by the time I handed it back
as was I.

change

after I met Kiki
everything changed
maybe if I wasn't in the depths of loneliness out there
I wouldn't have dived into that relationship
maybe I would have
but regardless of ifs and buts I did.

a chance meeting

we met in Harajuku
she was an actress and some kind of J-pop singer
I had never heard of her music or seen any of her films
she seemed to like that
at the end of the night she kissed me and ran away into a taxi
I went to a capsule hotel instead of waiting for the morning
train to Shisui
I had her number
but thought I'd never see her again
I met Mark and Ricky in Yoyogi park the next day to drink
cans and wander
she messaged asking if I was free
we met that night and almost every one after
and were living together within four months.

su-chan

Kiki had got a newborn kitten a few days before we met
wee Su-chan
abandoned
rescued from the cold floor of a factory by a worker
and she took him in
I was never that fond of cats before
but he was the best wee fella I ever met
she warned that he was prone to biting people
an angry wee fucker
but he never bit me
and we became best pals from day one
I'd wake up with him sleeping under my arm
and he'd follow me around her flat
in winter 2015 most days I was driving eight hours a day to get
to work and back
but it was worth it at that time
to see them both instead of an empty Shisui apartment
and when I finally got a university lecturing job
the hard hours paid off
those first 18 months with Kiki were like palm trees in the sun.

summer

dropped Su-chan off at her parents in the outskirts of Nagoya
and flew to Scotland for a two-week holiday
she met my family
we drove around a bit of the west coast
everything seemed fine
we went to see a play in the theatre with her favourite French
actress Juliette Binoche
she had an ambition to move onto plays
I had hoped this only strengthened that and her thoughts about
moving abroad
but I could see she was getting tired of speaking English
she got pissed off when we went to a café and the waitress was
from Manchester
and couldn't understand a word she said
I had adapted to a new culture in Japan
but that wasn't an easy thing to do
I saw how Japanese she was
and unwilling to change
wanted to sink back into an easier world where she was
important
would be impossible for her to live anywhere else
all talk of moving abroad at any point in the future went cold.

nhk

before I moved in with Kiki in Tokyo
I got a chap on the door in Shisui
a humid Monday night
pitch black
I was watching Celtic highlights on my laptop
half falling asleep
it was another NHK tv man
I'd had these wee bastards visit in fish town
and again in Shisui when I first moved in
I told him as nice as possible just as I did the others that I don't
watch NHK or have a tv
so I wasn't paying the license fee and goodnight
he gritted his teeth and was foaming with spit
said it was the law and I had to pay!
I must pay 200 quid there and then or he'd call the polis and
have me arrested
I said call them as that was a load of shite
as I went to close the door, he stuck his foot in
and tried to pull himself inside
I knew I was fucked if I even pushed him
but he wasn't getting inside my flat
I just put my weight against the door until he tired out
and pulled his wee shoe out in a fit of swearing
once he eventually fucked off, I locked the door
never answering it there again.

finally moving to actual tokyo

I was glad to see the back of Shisui
it had nothing going for it
there was no sinking feeling of sadness like I had in fish town
none whatsoever
it was like the relief of a first day at a new job finally being
over
I tried to get a parking space outside Kiki's flat in Setagaya-
Daita the day I moved
but the letting agent said the man who owned it didn't rent to
foreigners
Japanese only
same with every other owner in the area
although this was hardly a surprise given how openly racist
Japanese people were
this wasn't something I was prepared for
I had to go back and pretend it was Kiki's car
and after some convincing and paying three months upfront
I got to rent an overpriced tiny wee space in a fella's driveway
a 10-minute walk away
it was almost impossible to squeeze into
over 300 quid a month
but since I had to drive to the Chiba schools I had no other
option
it soured the move a wee bit
but life in Japan was never straightforward.

rainbow bridge

in Setagaya-Daita I had a much longer drive to work than from
Shisui
I'd wake up at 03:00
jump in the shower
feed Su-chan and run out
buy a hot chocolate and a big can of Mountain Dew from the
vending machine on the street heading to the car
by 03:30 I was in my car and heading for work
aiming to be there by 08:00 and get a quick half hour nap in a
combini carpark before starting
I drove down the hill to Shimokitazawa
and onto the dual carriageway under the bridge
swooped around the city and onto the Rainbow Bridge heading
for Chiba
if I was lucky I'd beat the trucks and have a good run
more times than not they'd take up both lanes and race at 50
kilometres per hour
the quicker I got there the longer my nap could be
I'd try to be out of Tokyo by sunrise
every day I'd see a major traffic accident
that would clog the roads
but one rare morning everything was going perfect
I had caught most of the lights
the trucks were easily passed
and I was out of the city in record time
the sun was rising through the tall buildings in a red glow
a beautiful drive at that time if you weren't in any kind of
hurry
I was weaving through the trucks on the motorway

listening to the American army radio station
a car behind was copying my movements
I smiled
same idea as me
until a siren blared and a loudspeaker told me to pull over
fuck
I had already maxed out my license by cutting over an orange
line a month earlier
if they took it I had no way to work
panic set in
I rolled down the window and the officer screamed for my
license
I fished it out and he disappeared to his car to check
came back with a form and threw the license at me
I said I didn't know Japanese
too fast! too fast!
I shrugged pretending not to understand
he gave up and the other fella came over
he pointed to the speedometer and pointed for me to put my
signature stamp on the fine
I said I don't speak Japanese and don't have a hanko stamp
couldn't sign it
they looked confused
this hadn't come up in their rule book
what to do if a foreigner didn't sign the fine?
they shouted, ripped up the paper, and sped off in front of me
I drove away, heart thumping against my ribcage
and pulled over into the next petrol station
took a different route on the side roads to avoid them
I was hardly speeding in that wee car
maybe looked bad compared to the slow trucks
but I got away with it.

japanese tv

walking in Shinjuku with Kiki after lunch
stopped by a Japanese tv crew for an interview
she wouldn't participate as it was against her contract
so I said I'd answer a few questions
of all the random interviews I did for Japanese tv this was the
strangest
they gave me a ball and showed two options
yes or no
and fired off some random questions about masculinity
their show was debating whether Japanese men should shave
their legs or not
I said I didn't but if they wanted to then go for it and chose yes
next their chests
again I said it didn't make them any less of a man if they
shaved their chests
I shaved mine in summer
they wanted me to open my shirt and show them
I told them to fuck off as this wasn't Baywatch
arms were next
I said again that was a little stranger but sure if they wanted to
then yes
the interviewer was jumping up and down
then he went on about clothing
this two-minute interview was going way over time
I told them men in Scotland wear kilts and showed him a photo
from my phone
he jumped up and down even more
he then asked if he could put make-up on my face
I declined and called it a day

I made a mental note not to stop when asked to be interviewed again.

midori

my Friday school was getting changed for a month
I was to go to a wee junior high school instead
as someone had quit there and the company didn't want to lose
the contract
I was to teach the midori class
I didn't know what a midori class was but said aye
I typed the school into the map and it was three hours away
which meant an extra hour in my bed
so already was a better option
I got there and was taken to a class with no chairs
the midori class was sitting on the floor
they were a lovely collection of all the special needs kids in the
school
separated and given their own year
seven in total
by then I had six months under my belt and knew exactly what
to do
the head of English must have been happy as she bought me a
cake the following week
of all the classes I had ever done, those were my favourite
I ate lunch with those weans every day
I passed wee Yuuki one of the boys with his mum on my way
home and waved
he was amazed to see that I existed outside of the school and
was hopping up and down
I gave them a lift home
and his mum took about 400 photos.

santa is magic

my company asked me to be Santa for a few nurseries
turn up, wave, and hand out a few presents to a few kids for an
hour
the suit would be provided
that was all
for an extra 200 quid
I had been Santa at my mum's nursery a few times and that
was easy so I agreed
I turned up and there was this wee suit that hardly reached my
shins and elbows and no beard
I walked out on to the stage waving
there were over 100 weans and parents and a tv camera filming
the Santa show
three nurseries had combined and were all in separate areas
with their own names
all wondering who the fuck this guy was
cos he was clearly not Santa
at 6'1, with gingery stubble and bags under my eyes from lack
of sleep,
I looked like a giant who had mugged Santa and stolen his
clothes
the host whispered in my ear the last Santa was magic, so
could I perform a few tricks?
I said I could play some Christmas songs on the piano that was
staring at me instead
but I sadly didn't know any magic
she said that would be perfect
I made up a few songs, singing the words Santa and Christmas
at random points

and finished with the Mortal Kombat theme song shouting
Merry Christmas at appropriate points
like a lunatic
and that went well
the fuck they knew any different
then after an applause I think I'm done
but she tells the audience
Santa is magic! and shhhushes them for my first trick
the only magic trick I could think of was making her teeth
disappear down her throat
instead I did the old pulling the thumb off trick to a thundering
applause
and bowed
I gave out the presents
and was ready to finally escape when the host jumps back on
stage
shhhushes them all again and said,
time to sing your Christmas song to Santa-san
and if Santa-san likes it he will dance!
so the weans sang a slow Santa-san song and all eyes and the tv
camera are on me to dance
I wondered what the fuck I was doing with my life
I began to dance like there was a wasp in my arsehole
they finally finished
but then it was a Q and A with Santa-san
I was given a microphone and all the weans' hands shot up to
ask questions
my Japanese was about to get tested to its fullest
the nursery staff were lovely lassies
and after gave me 40 quid worth of Uniqlo vouchers and some
cake to go home with
I never did see that 200 quid though
it was not an extra paying role I got informed months later
after a few emails

even though I had signed an additional contract for that
amount
I decided I was done with that company
and started to look into getting work at a university that night
I didn't think I had much of a chance
but even if it didn't work out, I was changing jobs in spring.

hokkaido

Hokkaido awaited for the new year
Su-chan went on the plane too as he wasn't getting left
anywhere this time
Kiki's father had a wee flat up there
rented a car and drove through the thick snow
beautiful place
hushed silence
far far away from the noise and swarming of people in Tokyo
we went ice skating on a frozen river
nothing open at night
new years eve stayed in
and watched the pineapple apple pen guy go around all these
variety shows
Japanese terrible tv at its best
almost as bad as the shite they churned out on the BBC
we visited a temple on new year's day
ate a soup curry
the snow forever falling
I could have lived there
made me realise I was getting sick of the big city
of constantly being around thousands of people
it also made me homesick for Scotland.

assistant professor

I had applied for two university teaching jobs in December
thought I'd try my luck now I had specific Japanese teaching
experience
couldn't keep up with the long distance driving to Chiba
my lower back was shivering with pain every night
and I wasn't renewing my contract
aside from the Santa fiasco, the money wasn't enough
I got two interviews from the two applications I sent
Meikai University got back to me the same day as the
interview
a nine-year contract starting in April
doubled my wages and half the hours
so I took that one
before finishing my PhD I had landed a great teaching post
ecstatic reading that email
one of the happiest moments of my life.

last of the last

Saahd called
instead of moving to Tokyo he was heading home
been three full years since we had landed in fish town
he had been working towards moving to Tokyo
but gave up as a job in banking was too hard to get
we went to Meguro to see the sakura trees over the river on his
last day
Kiki twisted into a bad mood early on
he was talking about being excited to be going back to London
and travelling in Europe again
I realised then she had no ambitions to ever leave Tokyo
or even leave Japan for any length of time
and wanted me to be the same
I waved him off at the train station
another chapter had ended
my original ties to fish town erased
sealed
and gone forever
every time someone I knew left I felt a pang of panic
as much as I liked my life in Tokyo
if I was with Kiki, was I always going to have to be there?
no option of ever going home
not even to somewhere in the north of Europe
early to mid 30s was a good time to be in that city
but older than that I was far from convinced
the silences between conversation on the way home widened
but I put those feelings aside and focused on my new job

things were going well in Tokyo
looking too far forward wasn't helping anyone.

five more times

I was lucky I didn't know what it was like to not have parents
both still alive
but were closing in on 60
driving home from my last day at school stuck in the usual
Tokyo traffic
I worked out that if I stayed in Tokyo and went home every
two years
and they lived to 70
I'd only see them five more times in my life
that thinking anchored me in the moment
I was too far away if I wanted that to change
I'd blink and my toddler nephews would be men
my sisters old
my brother a stranger
my parents long gone
five more times
it wasn't enough.

the dark side of japan

in Shinjuku train station I got off the train
on my way to changing lines
I went up one of the massive staircases
as the escalators were packed with commuters
about 50 steps
but everyone kept left
and the few going down stayed on the right
they kept to their system and I liked it
I saw a drunk salary man crossing over to the wrong side from
the top
plenty of room on his side but he seemed to want to barge
through everyone
a few people moved to the right to let him through
and I joined them not wanting to get in his way
as soon as he saw me he crossed back over
I couldn't hear what he was saying as I had headphones in
before I could get out of his way he shoved with everything he
had
I managed to grab the metal banister after stumbling back
down three steps
he laughed as he ran for a train
anger soured in my forehead
if I hadn't caught that pole I would have been lucky to have
survived
as usual no one even batted an eyelid to this
I added it to the mounting reasons why I was beginning to hate
that city and its people
he wasn't some rare crazy fucker
there was a deep-rooted hatred of foreigners in more than a

few people
the white vans at train stations shouting for the return of the
empire were common.

gaijin

the foreigners at Meikai that didn't have tenure were put in
another building
far away from the Japanese professors
if I had just arrived in Japan I would have found it strange
but it was just another unspoken Japanese thing
the blend of foreigners that found themselves in that university
worked well
Patrizia, the head of the department, an Italian-American
romance writer
and was as good a boss as I had ever come across
always willing to listen and give advice
and treated people well
Tyson, a Canadian in an Irish rebel band and did the rounds in
all the foreigner pubs in Tokyo
Nick, a New Zealander brought up in a hippy commune and
had a mispronounced Scottish surname Dalziel
Roy, an Australian DnD master that kept his real name a secret
for some reason
Jason, another Canadian was a quiet fella who ate more ice
cream in a week than the whole of Scotland did in July
Will, a Londoner who had a hard-on for Chomsky and Ainsley
Harriott
and Ben, another English fella who was soon returning home
after 15 years at almost 50
the pieces in the department fitted together
I honestly liked everyone
not one argument
being new to university teaching it was perfect
everyone was approachable

it might have been something to do with everything being so
far away from home
best place I ever worked in terms of co-workers.

come home

I went for lunch with Winn in Tokyo when his parents came to
visit
Vietnamese who immigrated to America
they were hoping he would leave Japan
worry carved into their aged faces
he didn't have any intention to
same local school job since he arrived five years before
when he went to the toilet
his dad said I should tell him to come back home
I told him later and he stayed silent
I don't think he ever will.

train to uni from setagaya daita

changing from driving that wee car to the trains was worse
than I had imagined
I needed to be on the first train of the day
06:40
any later there were no spaces
train one I had to squeeze on
summer the air was stinking
squashed against salary men with sweat lashing off them
still in full suits
until cool-biz season was declared
I'd be on that for 20 minutes to the busiest station in the world
Shinjuku
then crammed onto a train to Tokyo station for 30 minutes
then a good 20 minute march along the platform to catch the
final 24 minute train to Shin Urayasu
this train I got a seat and fell asleep
only a 20 minute walk to the uni from there
I'd buy a rice ball and grape juice from the station for
breakfast and hurry
at best I'd be drenched in my own sweat
at worst stinking of other people's
the uni gym didn't open until 10
I'd change in the toilets and dry off under the air con before
my first class at 09:00
the journey alone was mentally and physically draining.

moving flats

Mark was moving from Shinjuku to Shimokitazawa
one town over from where I was, which was great news
that Saturday morning I was shattered
but he needed help so I wasn't for letting him down
I slept in by an hour
but he hadn't started by the time I got over there at the back of
nine
the old flat was 19 floors up
took us a good few runs in the van
up and down and up and down for hours
once his stuff was dumped in the new place we went straight
for breakfast at about 15:00
a good wee Mexican restaurant in Shimo
with the food there was a nomihodai
all you can drink
I started on vodka cos I didn't fancy a beer on an empty
stomach
and was still drinking 12 hours later
could hardly walk
crawled home
and spun and spun in the bed until I passed out.

the death of the morning

in Alice Springs way back in 2006
I was in a pub after a tour through central Australia
noticing there was a group of us from Scotland the barman said
a national radio show was broadcasting from the pub that night
and asked if any of us would do the Braveheart speech for free
beer
the rest of the boys said naw
me like an eejit said aye fuck it why not
so I got up on the stage
pub's packed
and the radio fella hands me a mic
did I even know the Braveheart speech?
I thought I did
seen that film a hundred times
but my mind went blank
I heard a lassie near the front say 'aww'
I said anything that came into my head
and passed the mic back
died on my arse
no amount of free pints was worth it
when I woke up that morning after Mark's move to Shimo
that memory was swimming behind my eyes
and the day only got worse from then on
crippling hangover fear consumed me as I drank from the tap
in the kitchen
memories of kicking over bins
pissing in a lift
throwing a full can of beer into a building site
stealing an ornament from a pub

a whisky glass from another
hardly massive things
but I wanted to die
felt like the worst person in the world.

costco

I had promised to go to Costco with Winn the week before
he had come out at around 21:00 the previous night
and seeing since he'd driven six hours to Tokyo I couldn't say
no
I could hardly walk I was so hungover
I had a shower sitting down and got changed
Kiki had left for an audition
so I fed Su-chan and lay on the floor, waiting for Winn to drive
over
eyes pocketed with sleepglue
death whispering over my skin
I leaned against the shopping trolley when we got there
and waded through the swamp
he said he'd filmed me last night
pissing against a wall and singing
and he was going to post it on Facebook
cos it was funny
couldn't understand why I couldn't see the fucking funny side
and took some convincing not to
my hangover got worse
took me a full week to recover.

never going home

Tyson
Canadian fella at work
as good a man you could meet
attempted to renegotiate his marriage contract
all his money went to his wife
the Japanese way
he only got pocket money
less than his kids
the renegotiation failed
he yearned to go home one day
his wife said she was divorcing him once he stopped earning
he didn't know if she was joking or not
I hoped she was
would that have been my life 10 years on if I stayed in Japan?
the thought surfaced most sleepless nights
he always talked about going back home to Canada
but knew it was impossible.

trains in tokyo

punctual as fuck
but they sure would cram folk in
everyone slept on the train
no phone calls
no music without headphones
no eating
sleep even if you're only one stop away
all good rules
coming back from a night out
I saw a salary man think he was back home in bed
he had stripped off all his clothes and was lying on the train
floor naked
everyone ignored him
usually people could be passed out with their wallets hanging
out and no one touched them
but I saw folk being robbed
one man had fallen asleep with his wallet and phone in his
hands
another sitting across from him stood up, plucked them out
and got off the train before anyone could react
not that anyone would do anything anyway
people that gave old folk or pregnant women their seat were
foreigners
never saw one Japanese person give up their seat
not once in almost seven years
they all looked the other way when anything not concerning
them happened on the train.

weans

Nick sat across from me at work
loved Bali and used to go every summer
47 but just became a new father
said he wished he'd done it 10 years earlier
we were similar in many ways
so it made me think
Jason who was also in his late 40s just had his first child too
as did Roy who was my age
as did my youngest sister back home
it was fucking everywhere
I was 33 but hadn't given a family too much thought until then
bringing up a wean in Japan would have been difficult
especially if it was what they called a hafu
half Japanese half foreign
which mine would have been with Kiki
Roy worried about his wee boy being kidnapped
and while I thought that would have been extreme
the thought of having a mixed family in Japan was not
appealing.

the old left behind

Will started the same time as me
he would have a Viv and Bob or Matt Berry video waiting as I
got in from lunch
I only ever supported Celtic
and couldn't give two fucks about any other league than the
Scottish one
but he was the only person I could talk football with
even if it was the English league
and that was a home comfort of sorts
Ben sorted a weekend down the Chiba coast at Meikai's
summer house
a mansion with a private beach that uni employees could use
the three of us went and cycled around the coast
it was deserted
an old zoo that closed years before
reminded me of fish town
the youth departed for Tokyo
leaving the old to rot in the empty shells of villages
when Will left after two years, Patrizia offered me all of his
classes
which doubled my workload
they didn't want to try and recruit someone in a matter of
weeks
I knew it would be hard going
but the money was too good to turn down.

the funeral

during the summer break we got the bullet train to Kiki's
parent's house
full of relatives
all chain smoked
the house a cloud of grease and coughing
flowers everywhere
motorbike racing on the tv in the background
and they cheered for it like we would the football
some of her younger cousins even had scarfs
the wee granny was nice and said I used chopsticks well for a
gaijin when she was alive
the funeral was much more intense than one in Scotland
lasted three days
everyone had to say something to the body
then it was burned
I had to pick out a piece of jaw bone with chopsticks to put
with the rest of the unburned that were given to the grandfather
a Korean
who pretended to be full Japanese so his family wouldn't be
discriminated against
worked for the Yakuza but escaped
as nice a man you'd ever meet.

health check

coming back from Mikey's stag-do in Iceland
my health check test at the uni showed I had the liver and
kidneys of a 70-year-old
no more alcohol the doctor said no no no no no more okay?
no more
he was a funny old guy around 90
I had felt pain after only a few drinks in my sides
hangovers and anxiety were getting worse
a wake-up call
I cut down
hit the gym and the uni pool four nights a week
drank only water except on weekends
took me a few years
but in 2020 I had only three bottles of beer in total.

jehovah

a pack of Jehovah's Witness pricks turned up at the English
department social room
19-year-old brainwashed Americans
first time off their farms
thinking they were worldly and came to pretend to befriend the
awkward Japanese kids
when it was all a rouse to recruit them to the church
they were confident wee fuckers I'll give them that
chased out once Patrizia saw them
the following week one wee Japanese fella told me he was
going to the meetings at their church
to practise his English
he had a photo of a blonde girl
his new girlfriend he said
I saw another student with that same photo
his girlfriend too.

my parents came to visit

hardly ever venturing further than Spain
I never expected them to come
but they did that November and I was delighted
we went to a spa town in the mountains outside Tokyo
so they could experience a traditional Japanese hotel
the food was served in the room by an old woman who stared
to make sure you ate it
whole fish on sticks
raw fish
Japanese eggs
octopus balls
my mum tried but couldn't eat anything but the rice and
vegetables
they had a hard time sleeping on the tatami floor
but got a good idea of the life out there
opened both their eyes to a new world
to what was far beyond the outskirts of Glasgow.

kyoto

saw some temples and shrines
walked to see the monkeys on the mountain
I thought it would be peaceful
but there were guards whacking them if they went near people
even the wee baby monkeys
Korean BBQ for lunch went as well as the raw fish the
previous night
by the end of the day they were in McDonald's and there again
for breakfast
hardly ever ate it in Scotland but couldn't handle any Japanese
or Asian food
made me realise how different the food was and how different
my diet had become
I preferred eating rice and noodles more than chips most
nights.

saizeriya

they went for pasta every day after that at Saizeriya
a Japanese family restaurant chain
one that I went to a lot in fish town and Shisui
those kind of restaurants were life savers
open 24/7
decent food
and all you can drink soft drinks machine for under three quid
cheap
and had good chips
you can't go without chips for too long
even if you move to Tokyo and have the option of every kind
of food possible
it felt good to be able to speak normally again and hear
Scottish accents
not have to repeat myself over and over
and go back to speaking at a normal speed
the Americans had the hardest time understanding my accent
out of everyone I met
much more than the Japanese.

tourist

one of the best parts of living in Japan was having people visit
and I could be a tourist again
and take a break from the hectic working life
they could see the positives of living in Tokyo
I was a walk away from Shibuya and Shinjuku
near the big park
a great flat
the best wee cat
a great girlfriend
everything you could ever want around
except friends and family from back home
that was the only thing missing.

alone

it was the first time in my life I had spent any time with my
parents without my brother or my sisters being there
and after being apart for years
it was good to see them as people and not just parents
my mum cried as I took them to the train station
and that was hard to take
knowing there was a chance I'd never return to Scotland to live
again
I had a good job that paid well
I was settled with Kiki and she was in her final city
I couldn't see a future in Scotland anytime soon
if ever.

the salary man

I saw the salary man every day
same story written between the lines on his face as every other
early rise greeting the pale darkness
everyone asleep
scraped tiny white hairs off a worn face
parted his hair
and left the house
breathed the smoky morning haze
no seats on the Chiyoda Line left
everyone in silence
15 minutes to Hibiya
humidity burned
12 minutes to Tokyo Station
the office smelled of damp coffee
a meeting
desk work
a meeting
desk work
forced down the bento his wife prepared
hated ikura
hated horenso
hated tsukemono
never had the heart to tell her
desk work
tiredness burrowed up his spine and rests
lukewarm coffee in a plastic cup
a final meeting about tomorrow morning's meeting
darkness descended out from the window
pictured his wife when they were young

when there was love left in his heart
her heart
before the company became his everything
whether they wanted it to or not
sipped bitter lager at the izakaya
laughed at a joke that wasn't funny
the ikura the boss passes him was delicious
ate sipped smiled and laughed
ate sipped smiled and laughed
face stung from the effort
the Chiyoda line empty
everyone asleep when he returned
the bento box in the sink
crawled into bed
early rise greeting the pale darkness
everyone asleep
sat in the kitchen hands shaking
17 more years
204 more months
886 more weeks.

eddie

I met Eddie at work and we became good friends
he was part-time at the uni and floated in one day a week
a Korean fella who moved to Liverpool as a child
been in Japan for decades
knew everyone in Tokyo
he was always first to get drunk
usually two pints at most
and he'd steer the topic onto his bad luck with women
he had the worse luck
a lot of it his own fault
we went to a house party in Yoyogi once
he was getting along great with an English girl of Japanese
descent
they had lots in common and talked about going off for a drink
on their own
then he just walked off alone to get the train
in mid-conversation
I got a call 10 minutes later
he was coming back
made a mistake
but she had already left.

ueno

Eddie loved Ueno
any time we arranged to meet up he'd always suggest Ueno
and a standing bar that was at best a shit izakaya
we'd usually meet Don there
a wee fella with a Glasgow accent
but apart from four years at uni back home
lived almost all of his life in Japan
his mum was Scottish, dad Japanese
was like having a pal from back home
Ueno was a nice place but once you'd been you'd seen it all
we'd wander around the lake and the museums
Eddie would be excited to see things he'd seen a hundred times
then get some cans at the combini
I was on sangria in summer
pints of vodka at a Hub after the standing bar
before getting the last train home
Eddie was still in the same small town he first moved to 11
years ago
parents on the east coast of America
his sister on the west
he felt home was in England
but no one was there anymore
Japan was an easy routine of working and drinking like a lost
boy in Neverland
one he was marinated in.

living above an empty clothes shop

I moved to Yoyogi-Uehara with Kiki
a flat twice the size as the old one and near the park
with a big balcony that overlooked a garden
finally some space to breathe in
was great for wee Su-chan to run around in
of all the places I had stayed this was by far the best
Mark came to the town after work on a Friday
for a few drinks
we started in a whisky bar
then a crab bar that sold glasses of red wine for a quid
and went to quiet Irish bar that served Kilkenny
he took a sip of his pint and fell asleep
I closed my eyes for a long blink
woke up hours later
the pub was bouncing
I shook him and we fucked off
Fridays in those days were a right-off after nine
I had the energy of an 80 year old.

why him?

went to this 'showbiz' party in Meguro
spilling out onto the street
fake smiles dripping from the walls and into wine glasses and
plastic beer cups
I was the only foreigner there
Kiki was pointing out a famous director here and a famous
musician there
they all presumed I was an American actor
once I said I was a uni lecturer they weren't shy to end the
conversation
one guy who had proclaimed himself as Japan's greatest rapper
said to her,
so why him? you could get any Japanese guy you want
she laughed and the rest in the circle did too
it was just a Japanese thing, she told me when we got home
I had played gigs with a few Japanese bands on the line-up
all knew four chords between them
I went to one of her rehearsals before
and filled in on the piano
too classical, her guitarist said
and proceeded to show me with three fingers how to play an
instrument I was better than him at when I was 7
she had only ever dated actors, directors,
or famous musicians before
everyone around her seemed fake
friends only because they wanted something
she said that when she had collapsed and was in hospital for a
week no one visited.

what is, was, over

we had been together for over two years
and had settled in our Yoyogi-Uehara flat
Scotland had lost a last minute goal against England the night
before
I was sleep deprived, watching some shite film on the couch
with Su-chan
she was on the phone to her mum
a usual Sunday night
I was planning to have a shower and be in bed in an hour
she'd been on sleeping pills and was not long awake
back to smoking inside the flat with the extractor fan on
instead of going out to the balcony
something was up
she hung up the phone and wanted to talk
burst into a monologue
her dad had another affair with a hostess
her mum had threatened to commit suicide again
and... she'd had enough of me
the time bomb exploded
I was the reason why her career was slumping
I was the reason why she was sad
I was the real reason for everything going wrong
I was only going to ruin her life as her dad did to her mum's
I was in shock, wondering what the fuck was going on
then came the screaming
throwing things
I was in the midst of a nightmare with no way of waking
we were at the pictures and dinner the night before
not a whiff of any of her family or career problems being my

fault

I had to get out and it was over

we talked a little more but her mind was made

and welded closed

her face soaked in hatred

anger

she said she had to put her mum and her career first and I was
in the way

I was in shock and flooded in tears

she laughed

I didn't recognise who she had suddenly become

it was as if she was possessed

sure we'd had arguments in the past

but things usually sorted themselves out in a few hours at most

I went out for a walk to the combini to get my lunch for the
next day

when I got back she had calmed down

said she booked me a hotel near my uni

and that was it

the reality of it sank in

I could see she wasn't changing her mind

I stuffed clothes into a bag

trying to compose myself

Su-chan was running around the floor, thinking we were
playing a game

I walked out and closed the door.

monday

she blocked my number
I stayed late after work the next day
wondering what to do
I didn't want to go back to that hotel room
too tired for the gym
I sat at my desk and stared at the floor
thoughts eating flesh
mentally drained
bones ached from the lack of sleep
I walked the five minutes to the hotel and ran a bath
a case with my things had been posted to the hotel
and sat on the floor like an ulcer waiting to hatch
more sitting and thinking but in a tub of hot fucking water
I dunked my head under, hoping never to return
I had two double beds in the room
I lay across both, head pointed at the window
couldn't sleep
the room too hot or too cold
couldn't sleep
the grey dawn rose
I went to work.

after buying a pot noodle for dinner

I sat on the hotel bed at night
another suitcase had arrived with the rest of my things
signalling her decision was permanent
all my worldly possessions on the floor beside me
and watched the ticking of an old clock stuffed beside the tv
and aged and aged
curdled like rotting milk
her fading words cast shadows on the walls
I took one spoonful but couldn't force down another
I watched the new season of Twin Peaks on my laptop and
tried to sink into another world
I was still only 33 but felt over 60.

flying home

I got a new flat sorted a day or so before I had to fly back for
my brother's wedding
it had been a week and my thoughts were still sipping fire
an empty seat beside me on the plane
I tried to block out who should have been sitting there
back in Scotland the ground swallowed
I cast it aside so not to ruin anything for anyone else there
did my best man speech
and flew back the following morning
the nightmare night had lost its warmth but wouldn't quite fade
from memory
Edinburgh
London
Tokyo
and sank into an empty flat by the water in Urayasu
I should have seen it coming
there was a scratch of a feeling it would all sour
and run into dark drains
but I ignored it
and didn't look again until that scratch was a puss-filled
wound with flies drinking on the surface
there was something good between us without all the poison
that surrounded her
but even alongside that was a silently ticking time-bomb I
never quite heard.

darkness

I didn't have another get up in me
didn't have another start again left
like a never ending hangover
awake at 05:00
shallow sleep and headaches
I just wanted my life to be over
I couldn't see any future that I'd be happy even for a single
moment
mental health crumbling again
I continued to sink and sink and sink.

nekozane

my new flat was in Nekozane, Urayasu
a walk along the water away from Disneyland
ground floor with an upstairs storage area
I got a blow-up mattress and slept up there
I aged in those following months
withered
lost a lot of weight
took to drinking alone at home
something I had never done before
to give someone your complete trust
merge your life with theirs
build something
for it to crumble
rip the skin off and bleed
I was done
drowned
betrayal didn't cover it
it really didn't
I was so fucking lost
nothing made sense anymore
but as the days weeks and months passed
things got better.

surfing

I went to Niijima island with Winn at the end of the summer
for a few days
got an eight-seater plane to the island
while he took a choppy ferry ride
camped in a crowded site
he went out shooting fish on one side of the island
I went surfing on the other
well more like falling on my arse
and tumbling under the waves
there was a big outside onsen
I went alone late one night as Winn had made some Japanese
fish shooting pals
and another night of fishing chat in Japanese wasn't for me
an American from Hawaii was scaring people by trying to
perform miracles in the pools
a faith healer
it wasn't long before he was sitting across from me asking if I
feared his god
said there was a dragon in the Vatican
hated the Catholics
I said he'd fit right in with certain people in Scotland
I left when he decided to baptise me
then turned his attention to a group of Japanese teenagers.

sleepless

02:26
and still not asleep
thoughts drifted to faded memories of her
wordless
both long gone
I'd listen to Keaton Henson and drift away from those dreams
of a past lay dying
I never felt hate
always waiting for that day when anger would take hold
and hate would take over
but I never hated her.

six long months on

she called asking to meet
there was no one to look after Su-chan and he was sick
she had someone try to feed him while she was away filming
but he refused to eat
and had a cold
I took him back to my flat
and he was running around and eating again by the next
morning
she took him back three months later
and was like a changed person
said she'd booked us a spa for Christmas
said we can work things out
wasn't speaking to her family anymore
had made a mistake about us and was sorry
as if that was all that needed to be done
I was melting into the chair
you can't just throw someone away then expect they'll come
back whenever you want, I said to a silent reply
the lonely human fruit is always ripe for peeling, especially
wandering alone in a foreign land
but the last thing I needed
out of anything
was to get sucked back into her life
all I ever wanted in those first few months was what she was
offering there
but that time had passed
I wasn't going to take the risk that it wouldn't explode again
I'd be forever waiting for it
all trust was gone

no going back
the road was closed
forever
I was finally feeling better
we kept in touch
until we didn't.

neighbours

I first thought my neighbours upstairs were high school
students
cos they came back one night with school uniforms on
but saw later they were much older
and worked in a hostess bar
faces like damp floor rags
they would practise their singing in the flat
sometimes karaoke
sometimes without music
always screaming their lungs out at all hours
not giving a fuck
I had Su-chan over
so I knew if I complained they'd say I had a cat
as animals were banned in the building
my bed was in a loft part
right under their floor
two years of it.

windows

going home for Christmas
opened four windows in my ground floor flat to air the place
went for a shower
closed the curtains to get changed
zipped up my case
pulled my bike into the kitchen
and out
made sure the front door was locked
and headed for the airport with an all too familiar feeling that I
had forgotten something
but reassured myself that I hadn't
flat was locked
had my phone wallet passport
flew to London
then Glasgow
but still that feeling remained
I had left my bike outside in the spring and was lucky it wasn't
stolen
the two I had in fish town were
but that was definitely inside
it dawned on me that the windows were open
everything I had in the whole world was in that flat
and outside the windows a busy road
I wouldn't have been that stupid
shook that feeling off again
wouldn't have left them open
Christmas and New Year in Belfast passed
headed back two weeks later
when I got to my flat the curtains were blowing

half inside
windows wide open
felt the colour drain from my face
but by some miracle no one had went inside
only dirt and dead leaves had entered
Japan was safe
but there were thieves
phones, money, clothes, and iPads had gotten stolen at my uni
in that past year
lucky didn't cover it.

routine in urayasu

cycled to work
bought corn bread, alcohol-free cider, and a protein bar from
Family Mart
taught
slept at lunch, keeping up the tradition from the old teachers at
Togane
planned my classes
gym and swim
cycled home
wrote until I fell asleep
pizza on Thursday nights
salads and protein bars the rest of the week
repeat.

david

there was a new American fella at the university in my second
year
at first he couldn't understand a word I said
and would constantly joke about that
so I thought he was a right prick
as most of the Americans I had met in Japan were
but that wore away
he was one of the good ones
an interesting fella
former drug dealer from Seattle
growing up his dad only let him watch films from before the
1970s
the golden age
as he considered them wholesome
so he was right into old films and Elvis
he had a yellow house behind my flat with his wife and baby
we watched old films during the week
drank absinthe
and wandered far from the Urayasu shores.

disney princesses

I went on the online dating apps
mainly for something to do instead of eating dinner alone
every night
living next to Disneyland
and being the only straight single foreigner for miles and miles
I caught the attention of the American girls that worked as
Disney princesses
I went out on a date with one who was obsessed with how
famous she thought she was
how she had fans come see her no matter what character she
was playing
how she had to pretend to be in character on Instagram
how much they loved her
she talked and talked and talked
I had never met anyone so self-obsessed
didn't eat one slice of her pizza
she asked me to go see her perform at the closing parade
I didn't know what I wanted in my life
but knew it wasn't that.

groundhog day

not all the dates were bad
but even with the good ones I was bored of having the same
start up conversation over
and over again
where are you from?
how long have you been in Japan?
how long are you staying for?
how's your Japanese?
have you been to (place they're from) before?
it was like groundhog day
I was as bored of my answers and my stories as hearing theirs
and as much as I tried
I still had no interest in anyone else.

back in scotland in spring

was like walking around an old dream
nothing real
feeling only on the surface
shouldn't be there
it belonged to the past
decade almost over
as were the seconds in Japan
only a whisper remained
calling me back
for a final year.

last visitors from home

Bob and Phil
friends I'd known since school flew over
we spent the first day playing old games in the Akihabara
arcades
then to a Maid café for a laugh
ate ice cream in this creepy wee restaurant where wee lassies
pranced about in maid costumes
went to the Hub pub once it opened at 17:00 to wipe that
memory clean
Eddie and Laurence another English fella joined us for a few
an hour or so later a Japanese woman joined our table and
latched onto Phil
married
came straight from work
looking to meet a foreigner
he so strong so passion, she said
she sang from start to finish Toto's Africa in his ear
wrote inspirational messages on his hand like,
smile when you are sad
hand fed him fried spaghetti
even after five years Japan could still surprise me.

wandering

wandered around Tokyo
Yoyogi park
Tokyo Sky Tree
Senso-ji temple in Asakusa
karaoke in Shinjuku
Meguro river for the cherry blossom trees
a walk to Disneyland by my flat
ended up in a pub for opening time most days
the 300 yen bar in Ginza became one of my favourites
we went to a yakiniku restaurant, a meat bbq place in Urayasu
there was this wee fella behind us who had eaten half a cow
and was still shovelling it down
plate after plate after plate
that was the final time I ever ate cows
not because of that wee fella
many reasons
but mainly I couldn't justify in my head being against animal
cruelty and eating them
I taught a class of Chinese students at the uni
who asked all sorts of questions about the West
the Yulin dog eating festival was brought up in conversation
one of the students said it was no different to eating cows or
chickens
I had always separated animals into eating and non-eating
categories
that stayed with me
I thought about Su-chan and decided fuck it I was done
I was being a fucking hypocrite and knew it
it was a hard habit to stop

184

we went to this chicken restaurant the following night
best tasting I ever had
I tested myself not eating animals for a week
then a month
then never again.

going home

the morning Bob and Phil were about to leave Eddie turned up
at my flat
he came in and they were busy packing
told a story about how he went to a blowjob bar and took a
hooker to a love hotel
and bragged that since she was pregnant he managed to get a
discount
silence flooded the place
I don't know what reaction he expected
maybe being in Japan 11 years had smashed his senses against
a wall
they must have been wondering what sort of friends I had
made out there
but Eddie wasn't a bad person
far from it
he was as nice a fella as you could meet
and almost certainly made that up or heard that story from
another fella and said it was his
he did that sometimes
why I'll never know
taking Bob and Phil to the airport I wanted to be on that plane
and go home too
it was always great having people visit
and those were some of the best times I had in Japan
but going back to a cold empty flat alone
didn't appeal
their visit finalised my decision that I would be going home the
following year for good
no matter what.

bakery

there was this wee bakery next to the supermarket
always bouncing
I'd buy two rolls from there on Saturdays
and have wasabi crisps on them
can't beat a piece n crisps
and a bag of mixed nuts
C.C. Lemon
a bit of cheap dark chocolate
and that was me for the day
how the fuck I didn't drop dead I'll never know.

35

home from work
sat alone and ate a pineapple and jalapeño pizza
cold can of Dr Pepper
too tired to watch anything read anything
too awake to sleep
having a summer birthday I had spent a good few birthdays
travelling with my oldest friends
18 Spain in Benidorm on my last package holiday
19 Czech Republic in Prague on a three month tour of Europe
20 Thailand on our first real trip outside Europe
21 Holland in Amsterdam
22 Glasgow the day of my undergrad graduation
23 Australia in Brisbane on a year-long stay after finishing uni
27 Sweden in Stockholm
28 Slovakia at Pohoda music festival
the date was steeped in past memories
that I swallowed with each bite before setting an alarm for
07:00 and turned off my phone
34 I had a Burger King in that same flat in an almost identical
setting
I thought things would be different the following year
Nothing was going to change the longer I filtered out time in
that tiny flat on the banks of the Edo river
silence from a cold bed on the floor
cold walls
cold cold.

6th period writing class

classes were usually packed and difficult
but I had one writing class that was perfect
for students who failed their second year
and needed a make-up class
there were 24 students registered
two showed up in week one
a different two in week two
a mix of them in week three
a brand new boy in week four
then no one
ya dancer
I got paid to work on my own novel rather than help them with
theirs
the university was silent at night
best class I ever had.

neverland

one early Saturday evening
I met Mark and Ricky in Harajuku in this outdoor collection of
drink stalls
they were already steaming
celebrating almost buying a building
almost being the keyword
Mark had a bottle of red wine for breakfast to make the
meeting more interesting
negotiating buying a £1,000,000 block of flats while laughing
his heid aff
it didn't go ahead for some strange reason
only in Japan would I have considered a good drink before a
meeting a good idea
nothing actually felt truly real there.

fireworks

the big Tokyo fireworks every summer
the Japanese all got dressed up in their kimonos
and watched from the grass as different companies competed
for the best fireworks display
millions of people were there
my last summer
bucketing of rain
soaked and sweating from the humidity
trying to get drunk but can't
waded through the sea of people
train for half an hour
just to get to a pub that wasn't bouncing
never worth the hassle.

urayasu by the sea

Monday morning
winter wind whistled through cracks in the old flat
huddled under piles of blankets
felt like I hadn't slept an hour
hangover hatching and running out pores
turned the 07:30 alarm off
and sank eyelids for just a few more minutes
not yet willing to brave the cold
needed a hot shower to melt the ice clawing at bones
first lecture at 09:00 as usual
still had good time
up at 07:40 wouldn't hurt
woke again at 09:10
fuck
quick wash, grabbed my bag, and out the door
snow lashing
road swimming in slush
tried flagging down a taxi but they were all full
jumped on my bike and pulled up my hood
trousers and shoes soaking in minutes
peddled
along the main street
up the bridge
red raw hands
throat pouring blood
snap
fuck!
the chain was dangling by the back tyre
turned the bike upside down and got to fixing it

phone beeped with missed calls from my department
with palms and fingers coated in rust and oil, the chain was
back on
over the bridge and along the path
crossed the road
snap
FUCK
pushed and ran and pushed and ran
dumped the bike in the uni car park
blamed my lateness all on the broken chain
sat in the empty lecture hall
almost 10:00
first period students long gone
no lunch in my bag
wallet left by my fridge
starving
drenched
shivering
eight hours later back home
stared at the collection of empty beer cans that swamped the
sink
Sunday night drinking had to stop
and did.

nichiyobi

Sunday afternoons consisted of a half hour walk along the
Kyuedo river
to the Disney resort
full of American-style restaurants
I'd get a burrito and a donut
and go eat them sitting by the river
some days I'd be worn to a shadow with a hangover
but towards the end I'd all but given up the drink
gave me time to think and make a plan for coming home.

final year

didn't shave for over 11 months
became a challenge
every meal coated it
when I eventually shaved in November 2019 in Mark's flat in
Tokyo
and saw my old face again
it was like going back into a house you used to live in
different from what you remember
like when you wander into places from your past in a dream
felt strange for days after
weeks even.

oishii

showed a first year undergrad class the Earthlings
documentary
so they could think from another perspective
not just the Japanese 'eat all the animals' one
one girl said delicious when the dolphins were being
slaughtered on the harbour
tasty animals
after some class debate
they didn't see it as cruel
the fishermen needed to work
that was a good job
no one sided with the dolphins
I gave up.

nippon

Japan
a soup full of blatant racism
disregard for anyone but themselves
disrespect towards their elderly and women are almost second
class citizens
and ruthlessness
yet within all that
the culture is full of respect and manners
the people are the some of the kindest you could ever meet
friendliest
most hospitable
a strange place
nowhere like it in the world.

relationships

I had met other women since I broke up with Kiki
and some were nice lassies
but I couldn't be with anyone else
I tried but couldn't
took me a long time to get over her
there was always something stopping me from moving on
it was only after a random meeting in Singapore I realised I
had finally let her go.

everyone else hasn't a chance

in my penultimate year I met a girl in Singapore
on my way back home for the summer to meet my brother and
his wife there
she was from Wales and had lived there for four years with no
intention of leaving
I thought nothing would come of it
but we kept in touch
she came to visit Japan that October
we went to Bali in November
Scotland and Norway in December
the tide just kept flowing in the right direction
I went to stay with her in Singapore after I left Japan at the end
of March
we went to Malaysia, Borneo, and the Philippines in April
Croatia in June
October stayed with her in Singapore for a month as she
decided to leave
went to Hong Kong in November to meet her brother
New Zealand in December
Wales in January
by February we had a flat together in Edinburgh
a week before the covid-19 virus forced us into lockdown
from one extreme to the other
but it worked out
sometimes these things do
everything I did in Japan led me to her
so I don't regret a single thing
we were engaged in August 2020.

only days remained

by March I had finished teaching at the university
arranged my moving out date
and gave everything away I couldn't take home on Mottainai
by the last week all that was left was a mattress on the floor
I had Su-chan for my final two months
was difficult to hand him back
but I clung onto the hope I'd take him to Scotland one day
I went to Hiroshima for my final few days
somewhere I had always wanted to visit
wandering around alone in a strange city
brought me back full circle to my first days in Osaka
I felt a sea of time between those days
so much had happened
so much had changed within me.

last night

last night living in Japan
crushed by memories
ready to break down
but holding on
no idea what the future would hold in Scotland
no idea
excited
but dreading once the gates were locked and the novelty of
being home went away
it was hard going at times
but worth the experience
I got the train to the airport, checked-in, and sat in the
departure gate lost in thought
my life as I knew it was over.

About the Author

John Gerard Fagan is a Scottish writer from Muirhead in the outskirts of Glasgow, who currently lives in Edinburgh. He has published close to a hundred short stories, essays, and poems in Scots, Scottish Gaelic, and English. *Fish Town* is his first book, detailing his life in Japan from 2013-2019.

The cover art is a painting called 'Forever Lost' from 2005, painted by John on an old record sleeve.

For more information visit: johngerardfagan.com
Or on Twitter: @JohnGerardFagan

About Guts Publishing

Established in May 2019, we are an independent publisher in London. The name came from the obvious—it takes guts to publish just about anything. We are the home to the freaks and misfits of the literary world.

We like uncomfortable topics. Our tagline: Ballsy books about life. Our thinking: the book market has enough ball-less books and we're happy to shake things up a bit.

Fish Town (Apr 2021) is our second memoir and John's debut. We are delighted to bring this story to you and hope you've enjoyed reading it. Well done John Gerard Fagan.

Euphoric Recall (Oct 2020), our debut memoir, is the story of a Scottish working-class lad and his recovery from addiction and trauma. Well done Aidan Martin.

Sending Nudes (Jan 2021) is our third anthology. A collection of fiction nonfiction and poetry uncovering the various reasons people send nudes.

Cyber Smut (Sept 2020), our second anthology, is a collection of fiction, nonfiction and poetry about the effects of technology on our lives, our sexuality and how we love.

Stories About Penises (Nov 2019) is our debut anthology. A collection of fiction, nonfiction and poetry about, well, exactly what it sounds like. To quote a prominent Australian author, 'Quite possibly the best title of the year.' We think so too.

Our website: gutspublishing.com.
Our email: gutspublishing@gmail.com

Thank you for reading, and thank you for your support!

9 781838 471903